"I am elated to be able to  Worship and Self Reflect pilation you did on Facet praying, and seeking gu prepared you. You have this auspicious opportunity to pen this devotional which will bless many and assist us all in how to self-reflect, expose, and get honest about hidden sins and struggles. This book is going to assist many in their search for a pure relationship with Christ. Blessings to you for you have experienced the subject matter through the Spirit and that qualifies you to be a formidable, qualified teacher of the subject matter along with your being Called, Anointed, and Appointed by the Lord."

Apostle T.A. Holman,
Sr. Founder, Prelate, CEO
Thee House of God in Christ Inc. Int.
Denmark, SC

It is with distinct honor and privilege I write this endorsement for 30days of pure worship and self -reflection. As your pastor, I could not be even more proud of your accomplishments as a Kingdom Scribe. This book is truly reflective of the lifestyle you live. You are definitely a worshipper and live a life of self-reflection. This book is also reflective of your relationship and undying love for our Lord and Savior Jesus Christ! You should be proud and please know your Pastors are extremely proud of you.

Respectfully Submitted
Overseer Curtis and Dr. Kia Everett,
Pastors of Destiny Christian Worship Center

30 Days of Pure Worship and Self Reflection is a transformational devotion. Pride was one of my favorite topics because I love how the author gave not only a great biblical example of where pride can lead us, but she was transparent about her own struggles with pride. This devotional was so relatable to me. I enjoyed the solutions and words to chew on sections provided by the author which really helped me to reflect even more on my own personal struggles.

Teresa Satchell, Raleigh, North Carolina

I have had the blessing of working with Nayjuana Stephens for two years. She coordinates and leads a time of scripture-focused prayer each week for a small group of warriors who need fortification in the midst of highly stressful circumstances. She lives and breathes the truth of what she has shared in this devotional. I love the flow of each day as she leads us from entering into worship with a song to the ending with a final prayer. Every day is a complete meal for the believer to meditate on. One excerpt, which really pierced my soul, was Day 5, entitled, "Complaining." Teaching middle school is extremely challenging, and my tendency is to complain. The final prayer of that day's entry is one I will pray daily as I enter into the battle, "activating the power that is within me" and "speaking life into my situation." Day 17, "Spiritual Distraction" is another theme that really speaks to me. I believe it is a good word for many others as well in this era of digital distraction. We all have a bit of Martha in us, but we need to cultivate our Mary side, taking the time to sit with Jesus and listen to his words to us. Nayjuana's "30 Days of Pure Worship and Self-Reflection" is a tool that will help us to do just that.

Heather Musselman, Pennsylvania

30 Days of
Pure Worship
and Self Reflection

1/28/2019

*May God bless you
in all of your endeavors!*

~Najuana C. Stephens

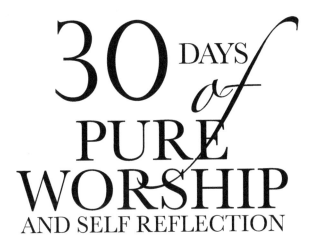

30 DAYS *of* PURE WORSHIP

AND SELF REFLECTION

A GET HONEST DAILY DEVOTIONAL FOR YOU

NAYJUANA C. STEPHENS

XULON PRESS

Xulon Press
2301 Lucien Way #415
Maitland, FL 32751
407.339.4217
www.xulonpress.com

Unless otherwise indicated, Scripture quotations taken from the English Standard Version (ESV). Copyright © 2001 by Crossway, a publishing ministry of Good News Publishers. Used by permission. All rights reserved.

Printed in the United States of America.

ISBN-13: 978-1-54564-128-6

First, and foremost, without my Lord and Savior Jesus Christ this devotional book would not exist, so this book is dedicated to the ministry and work for the building of the Kingdom of God. All that I have belongs to Him; "It is in Him that I live, move, and have my being." Acts 17:28

In loving memory of my father, the late Reverend Tyrone Woodberry, Sr. (September 3, 1955-August 14, 1991), I dedicate this book as a legacy for the love, faith, discipline, and support he has instilled in me. My father worked full time as a social worker, was a pastor, went to school, and was heavily involved in the community; yet, he always made time to be with his family and attend every one of my events that I was involved in from sports, music, drama and more.

TABLE OF CONTENTS

ACKNOWLEDGMENTS

To my loving and supportive husband, Kevin, thank you for allowing me to do ministry. You are my quiet strength behind all that I do. To my children, Krisalyn and Christopher, thank you for your love and the sacrifices you've made for the sake of ministry. I'm so proud of you and the talents and gifts God has displayed in you. To my mother, Nellie, who has always believed in me. A huge thank you to my pastors, Overseer Curtis and Dr. Kia Everett for their godly teachings and for seeing the greater in me.

INTRODUCTION

A re you a someone who has secret sinful behaviors that no one knows about? Do you find yourself repeating the same sins over again? Do you want to overcome areas in your life that are keeping you stuck and from experiencing the presence and power of God?

Let your eyes be opened about the real you as you explore areas of sin that have manifested in your life.

Let's get free from bondage.

I wrote this devotional because I've struggled and have seen others struggle in many areas of sin. We were blind to truth. Throughout ministry, I've also seen many people fall into sin. Many people wear a lot of masks and one of them is not being honest about our faults. We are guilty of believing in God, but not His power and live a lifestyle as though He does not exist. It's difficult for many Christians to get into the presence of God and yet not fulfill our destiny because of "our stuff" or areas in our lives that we have not surrendered to Christ. Over the years, as I spent time with the Lord and really got honest with myself, the Holy Spirit revealed areas that I had to repent of.

(The devotional 30 Days of Pure Worship and Self Reflection is an honest daily devotional for Christians that provides tools for self-evaluation intended to draw Christians closer to Christ through worship, repentance and the Bible. This devotional is written for Christians to deepen their relationship with Christ. This devotional will show you the power of God while helping the reader get into the presence of God and fully surrender to Christ. Each daily devotional includes suggested music, selected BIBLE passages, problems in the world, solutions to those problems, and a daily prayer.)

Day 1

SELF-RIGHTEOUSNESS

<u>Song:</u> "You Deserve It" J.J. Hairston

<u>Scripture Reference(s):</u> Matthew 1:17-25; Acts 1:1-3

17 So all the generations from Abraham to David were fourteen generations, and from David to the deportation to Babylon fourteen generations, and from the deportation to Babylon to the Christ fourteen generations.
18 Now the birth of Jesus Christ took place in this way. When his mother Mary had been betrothed to Joseph, before they came together she was found to be with child from the Holy Spirit. 19 And her husband Joseph, being a just man and unwilling to put her to shame, resolved to divorce her quietly. 20 But as he considered these things, behold, an angel of the Lord appeared to him in a dream, saying, "Joseph, son of David, do not fear to take Mary as your wife, for that which is conceived in her is from the Holy Spirit.

21 She will bear a son, and you shall call his name Jesus, for he will save his people from their sins." 22 All this took place to fulfill what the Lord had spoken by the prophet:

23 "Behold, the virgin shall conceive and bear a son, and they shall call his name Immanuel"

(which means, God with us). 24 When Joseph woke from sleep, he did as the angel of the Lord commanded him: he took his wife, 25 but knew her not until she had given birth to a son. And he called his name Jesus. (Matthew 1:17-25)

"And Saul approved of his execution.

And there arose on that day a great persecution against the church in Jerusalem, and they were all scattered throughout the regions of Judea and Samaria, except the apostles. 2 Devout men buried Stephen and made great lamentation over him. 3 But Saul was ravaging the church, and entering house after house, he dragged off men and women and committed them to prison. "(Acts 1:1-3)

Problem In The World: Many Christians believe in God, but live as though God doesn't exist. Gary Groeschel, in his book, The Christian Atheist, gives a vivid picture of true hypocrisy in the body of Christ. In other words, many of us have a form of godliness and yet we deny the very power of God. (II Timothy 3:5-7)

During the campaign of President Elect Donald Trump in 2016, there were many who expressed hostile feelings toward him because of his blatant stance on immigrants, women, minorities, foreign policy, and more. Likewise, there were those who opposed the views of Hilary Clinton and for her involvement in an FBI investigation for sending correspondence from her private email account as the Secretary of State, money laundering, and cover up for former President Bill Clinton's sex scandal.

Problem in the Text: Saul had men, women, and children dragged out of their homes to be killed for professing or believing in Christ. Saul gave his approval for a devout Christian, Stephen, to be stoned to death.

Solution to the Text: Christ came 42 generations for all people! He descended from people who were of unpopular opinion: he came from ordinary people who were murderers, adulterers, liars, idol worshippers, whoremongers, and the lusts of the flesh that scripture talks about. Christ the Messiah came for all men: Saul martyred Christians, but he had an encounter with Christ and his name was changed to Paul. How much more will Christ do for you and change you?

Solution to the World: In the 2016 presidential campaign, there was a video that showed President

Trump being prayed for by seven to ten Christians who laid hands on him. Moments later, another video was shown of a pro-Trump supporter shouting and chanting loud and clear Trump's name while on board an airplane. Ironically, no one on the aircraft protested the chants. Regardless of how one may have felt about either of the candidates (Hillary Clinton), too often we look down on people whom we think don't deserve Christ's love. Romans 5:8 assures us that, "While we were yet sinners, Christ died for [you] us."

Words to Chew On: Unfortunately, we are unable to fulfill the call on our life because we haven't truly examined our hearts and got gut level honest with God about "our stuff." There are areas in our life that we need to totally surrender to God, self -righteousness is one of them. "Judge not, that you be not judged. 2 For with the judgment you pronounce you will be judged, and with the measure you use it will be measured to you. Matthew 7:1-2. Salvation would be pointless if Christ came from heaven, lived on earth, bled and died on the cross for only a select few. We would not know the amazing power of God's saving grace to transform lives.

Prayer: Father, I repent for thinking of myself more highly than I ought. You said in your Word that "there is none righteous and that all have sinned and fall short of your glory." (Romans 3:23). Help me to see others as you see them. Help me to extend the same measure of grace that you have shown me, to those I deem undeserving of grace. I bind the spirit of pride in me that would cause self- righteousness to rise up in me to think that you died only for me. Loose a spirit of love. Holy Spirit, increase in me and allow self to decrease in Jesus' Name. Teach me how to love, [for] "…there is salvation in no one else, for there is no other name under heaven given among men by which we must be saved." (Acts 4:12) Thank you, for your cleansing power. Amen.

Day 2

PRIDE

Song: "Praise Jehovah" Beverly Crawford

Scripture Reference: Daniel 4:28-33

28 All this came upon King Nebuchadnezzar. 29 At the end of twelve months he was walking on the roof of the royal palace of Babylon, 30 and the king answered and said, "Is not this great Babylon, which I have built by my mighty power as a royal residence and for the glory of my majesty?" 31 While the words were still in the king's mouth, there fell a voice from heaven, "O King Nebuchadnezzar, to you it is spoken: The kingdom has departed from you, 32 and you shall be driven from among men, and your dwelling shall be with the beasts of the field. And you shall be made to eat grass like an ox, and seven periods of time shall pass over you, until you know that the Most High rules the kingdom of men and gives it to whom he will." 33 Immediately the word was fulfilled

against Nebuchadnezzar. He was driven from among men and ate grass like an ox, and his body was wet with the dew of heaven till his hair grew as long as eagles' feathers, and his nails were like birds' claws.

Problem in the World: Too often, many people think that their accomplishments or successes were achieved on their own strength, apart from God. Many hold the view that their titles, degrees, looks, money in their bank account, the car(s) they drive or the houses they live in came about from their own doing. People have made man and material things their god and have worshipped them rather than the Creator.

Problem in the Text: King Nebuchadnezzar was known as the builder of cities. In fact, he thought of himself as one of the gods in that he made an image of himself for people to bow down and worship it whenever a certain music was played. He tended to forget the demonstrations of God's power he had witnessed with Daniel and his friends, who refused to bow down to the image, who were not burned when he had them thrown into the fiery furnace.

Solution to the Text: In the first couple of chapters of Daniel, King Nebuchadnezzar decreed that whenever the music played that everyone should bow and worship his golden statue. God revealed his power when he saved Daniel and his friends from the lions' den and fiery furnace when they disobeyed the king's order. King Nebuchadnezzar experienced seven years of insanity in that he ate grass like an animal, his fingernails grew long like bird claws, and his hair and beard grew long. King Nebuchadnezzar had to be brought low for him to call on the Lord. Eventually, King Nebuchadnezzar recognized the sovereign God and said, "All those who walk in pride, God is able to put down." (Daniel 4:37). Kings and rulers too are subject to God Almighty. "As I live, says the Lord, every knee shall bow to me, and every tongue shall confess to God." (Romans 14:11)

Solution to the World: What do you do when everything has been taken away from you and you are put in a position where you have to trust God only? Surprisingly, there are pastors and leaders who are "busy doing the work of the Lord," and who rely on their own strength and intellect, and yet they neglect spending time in the very presence of the Lord with prayer and fasting, or in praise and worship or seeking the Lord's will for guidance.

I am a witness to many of the mindset that: "I can do it all by myself and I don't need God's help." Earlier in my career, I was introduced to my very first small business opportunity while working a full-time job. I was doing quite well with the business venture; (so

I thought) but, not well enough to retire from my full-time job in hopes that the business opportunity would supersede my full-time income. My attitude was boastful whenever I shared with others my early retirement. Needless to say, I found myself applying to and working at odd jobs (in the social work/education field) that were below my skilled qualifications, just to make ends meet. What a humbling experience! In hindsight as I reflect now, like King Nebuchadnezzar, I too had to be broken down. The Lord showed me that had I consulted him and not leaned to my own understanding, he would have shown me, "it is He who gives me the power to get wealth." (Deuteronomy 8:18) and if I, "Call to [Him] me and I will answer you, and will tell you great and hidden things that you have not known." (Jeremiah 33:3) Thank God, Romans 5:8 tells us that, "While we were yet sinners [and saved by grace], Christ died for us."

Words to Chew On: We must recognize that no matter how great we think we are, "It is He who made us and not we ourselves," (Psalm 100:3). Also, we must recognize that in all that we do or in our successes "… apart from Christ we are nothing." (John 15:5)

God is looking for a people who has a broken and repentant heart (Psalm 51:17); Without relying on the supernatural power of God, we defeat ourselves.

God is willing and able to work on our behalf but we have to lay aside the sin [of pride] that so easily entangles us. (Hebrews 12:1) Circumstances that we may have placed ourselves or others in that doesn't quite go the way we planned have a way of bringing us to our knees and crying out to God in humble sub-mission. "If my people who are called by my name, will humble themselves and seek my face and turn from their wicked ways, then I will heal their land." (II Chronicles 7:14). Even in the error of our ways and in our stupidity, "we were bought with a price." (I Corinthians 6:20)

Prayer: Holy Spirit, I know that pride is what turned Satan and the fallen angels from you. I acknowledge that pride is not of you. Please forgive me for leaning unto my own understanding and for allowing pride to consume me. Forgive me for not acknowledging that your thoughts are higher than my thoughts and your ways higher than mine. (Isaiah 55:8-9). Remove the spirit of pride from me. Help me to come to you with a broken and contrite heart Psalm 51:17. I ask you for spiritual healing in my thoughts, attitudes, and speech that it will reflect a true worshiper of Christ. May I truly know the God who redeems and not mer-rily know *of* the Redeemer. Thank you, for your blood that purifies. Seal this prayer In Jesus' Name. Amen.

Day 3

INTEGRITY

Song: "Create in Me A Clean Heart" Donnie McClurkin/ Maranatha Singers (Psalm 51:10)

Scripture Reference(s): II Samuel 11-12, Psalm 51

In the spring of the year, the time when kings go out to battle, David sent Joab, and his servants with him, and all Israel. And they ravaged the Ammonites and besieged Rabbah. But David remained at Jerusalem.

2 It happened, late one afternoon, when David arose from his couch and was walking on the roof of the king's house, that he saw from the roof a woman bathing; and the woman was very beautiful. 3 And David sent and inquired about the woman. And one said, "Is not this Bathsheba, the daughter of Eliam, the wife of Uriah the Hittite?" 4 So David sent messengers and took her, and she came to him, and he lay with her. (Now she had been purifying herself

from her uncleanness.) Then she returned to her house. 5 And the woman conceived, and she sent and told David, "I am pregnant."

6 So David sent word to Joab, "Send me Uriah the Hittite." And Joab sent Uriah to David. 7 When Uriah came to him, David asked how Joab was doing and how the people were doing and how the war was going. 8 Then David said to Uriah, "Go down to your house and wash your feet." And Uriah went out of the king's house, and there followed him a present from the king. 9 But Uriah slept at the door of the king's house with all the servants of his lord, and did not go down to his house. 10 When they told David, "Uriah did not go down to his house," David said to Uriah, "Have you not come from a journey? Why did you not go down to your house?" 11 Uriah said to David, "The ark and Israel and Judah dwell in booths, and my lord Joab and the servants of my lord are camping in the open field. Shall I then go to my house, to eat and to drink and to lie with my wife? As you live, and as your soul lives, I will not do this thing." 12 Then David said to Uriah, "Remain here today also, and tomorrow I will send you back." So Uriah remained in Jerusalem that day and the next. 13 And David invited him, and he ate in his presence and drank, so that he made him drunk. And in the evening he went out to lie on his couch with the servants of his lord, but he did not go down to his house.

14 In the morning David wrote a letter to Joab and sent it by the hand of Uriah. 15 In the letter he wrote, "Set Uriah in the forefront of the hardest fighting, and then draw back from him, that he may be struck down, and die." 16 And as Joab was besieging the city, he assigned Uriah to the place where he knew there were valiant men. 17 And the men of the city came out and fought with Joab, and some of the servants of David among the people fell. Uriah the Hittite also died. 18 Then Joab sent and told David all the news about the fighting. 19 And he instructed the messenger, "When you have finished telling all the news about the fighting to the king, 20 then, if the king's anger rises, and if he says to you, 'Why did you go so near the city to fight? Did you not know that they would shoot from the wall? 21 Who killed Abimelech the son of Jerubbesheth? Did not a woman cast an upper millstone on him from the wall, so that he died at Thebez? Why did you go so near the wall?' then you shall say, 'Your servant Uriah the Hittite is dead also.'"

22 So the messenger went and came and told David all that Joab had sent him to tell. 23 The messenger said to David, "The men gained an advantage over us and came out against us in the field, but we drove them back to the entrance of the gate. 24 Then the archers shot at your servants from the wall. Some of the king's servants are dead, and your servant Uriah the Hittite is dead also." 25 David said to the

messenger, "Thus shall you say to Joab, 'Do not let this matter displease you, for the sword devours now one and now another. Strengthen your attack against the city and overthrow it.' And encourage him."
26 When the wife of Uriah heard that Uriah her husband was dead, she lamented over her husband. 27 And when the mourning was over, David sent and brought her to his house, and she became his wife and bore him a son. But the thing that David had done displeased the Lord. (II Samuel 11:1-27)
1 "And the Lord sent Nathan to David. He came to him and said to him, "There were two men in a certain city, the one rich and the other poor. 2 The rich man had very many flocks and herds, 3 but the poor man had nothing but one little ewe lamb, which he had bought. And he brought it up, and it grew up with him and with his children. It used to eat of his morsel and drink from his cup and lie in his arms, and it was like a daughter to him. 4 Now there came a traveler to the rich man, and he was unwilling to take one of his own flock or herd to prepare for the guest who had come to him, but he took the poor man's lamb and prepared it for the man who had come to him." 5 Then David's anger was greatly kindled against the man, and he said to Nathan, "As the Lord lives, the man who has done this deserves to die, 6 and he shall restore the lamb fourfold, because he did this thing, and because he had no pity."

7 Nathan said to David, "You are the man! Thus says the Lord, the God of Israel, 'I anointed you king over Israel, and I delivered you out of the hand of Saul. 8 And I gave you your master's house and your master's wives into your arms and gave you the house of Israel and of Judah. And if this were too little, I would add to you as much more. 9 Why have you despised the word of the Lord, to do what is evil in his sight? You have struck down Uriah the Hittite with the sword and have taken his wife to be your wife and have killed him with the sword of the Ammonites. 10 Now therefore the sword shall never depart from your house, because you have despised me and have taken the wife of Uriah the Hittite to be your wife.' 11 Thus says the Lord, 'Behold, I will raise up evil against you out of your own house. And I will take your wives before your eyes and give them to your neighbor, and he shall lie with your wives in the sight of this sun. 12 For you did it secretly, but I will do this thing before all Israel and before the sun.'" 13 David said to Nathan, "I have sinned against the Lord." And Nathan said to David, "The Lord also has put away your sin; you shall not die. 14 Nevertheless, because by this deed you have utterly scorned the Lord, the child who is born to you shall die." 15 Then Nathan went to his house.

And the Lord afflicted the child that Uriah's wife bore to David, and he became sick. 16 David therefore sought God on behalf of the child. And David fasted and went in and lay all night on the ground. 17 And the elders of his house stood beside him, to raise him from the ground, but he would not, nor did he eat food with them. 18 On the seventh day the child died. And the servants of David were afraid to tell him that the child was dead, for they said, "Behold, while the child was yet alive, we spoke to him, and he did not listen to us. How then can we say to him the child is dead? He may do himself some harm." 19 But when David saw that his servants were whispering together, David understood that the child was dead. And David said to his servants, "Is the child dead?" They said, "He is dead." 20 Then David arose from the earth and washed and anointed himself and changed his clothes. And he went into the house of the Lord and worshiped. He then went to his own house. And when he asked, they set food before him, and he ate. 21 Then his servants said to him, "What is this thing that you have done? You fasted and wept for the child while he was alive; but when the child died, you arose and ate food." 22 He said, "While the child was still alive, I fasted and wept, for I said, 'Who knows whether the Lord will be gracious to me, that the child may live?' 23 But now he is dead. Why should I fast? Can I bring him back again? I shall go to him, but he will not return to me." (II Samuel 12:1-23)

<u>Problem in the World</u>: C.S. Lewis said, "Integrity is doing the right thing when nobody is looking." Many people, including leaders lack integrity in business deals, marital issues, family/friend relationships, and more. On a scale of 1-10 where are you in your walk with the Lord today? A ten meaning that you are on a mountain top experience and a one meaning that your walk with Christ needs a lot of work and that you need to urgently spend time in prayer and reading the Word of God. I would even venture to say that you may need to accept Christ into your life or recommit your life to him if it has been at a low for several days. Reverend, Dr. David Buschman asked me this question when I first entered college. Until that point and even now, no one had challenged my faith and gave me a gut level check like that. Many Christians are used to being superficial. We know how to speak Christianese: say words and prayers that sound super spiritual or dance a "holy dance" when the right music is played. What is your character like apart from when you are in a church setting? Too often, we make decisions without fully considering the ramifications it will have on us later or the impact it will have on others. It's easy to appear righteous before others, but can you honestly say that in your business dealings, family or work relationships, and day to day operations that you have pure motives? What is your character like? What do you think people at

your job will say about you? How about your family? Who are you when no one else is looking?

Problem in the Text: David, *the king,* could have anything he wanted. People entrusted their lives to him, like Uriah, his loyal friend. Of all the women that King David could have sexual relations with, did he have to sleep with, Bathsheba, his best friend's wife? To make matters worse, Bathsheba became pregnant with David's child. He tried to cover up his adulterous affair by attempting to get Uriah to have sexual relations with Bathsheba, so it could look like the unborn child was naturally Uriah's. David resorted to having Uriah killed by placing him at the front line of battle when Uriah opted to serve the king rather than lay with his wife. David had Uriah killed so that he could save face and not appear unrighteous before the people he ruled as the king.

Solution to the Text: David messed up big time, but the Lord still showed that, he had a plan and purpose for David and the Lord still wanted to use him as king because the King of Kings would come from David's line. Jesus' earthly father, Joseph, demonstrated that he was a man of integrity. When Joseph found out that his fiancée, Mary, was (supernaturally impregnated by the Holy Spirit) pregnant (and he knew the child was not his), he thought to secretly put Mary away rather than divorce her and make a public spectacle of her. Joseph soon recognized through a revelatory dream that Mary would give birth to the Holy Child, Jesus. David showed godly sorrow in Psalm 51. David's sin didn't stop the Savior of the world from entering the world to redeem mankind.

<u>Solution to the World:</u> I was reminiscing with a pastor friend how we planned sin in our earlier years while still serving in ministry, attending Christian conferences and still going to church and praising God. In fact, I recall serving in an inner city, particularly, for missions. Imagine my shock when I heard of rumors and I saw with my own eyes, married and single pastors/leaders at this conference bringing women (some from the conference) to their hotel rooms. Perhaps, I was naïve to think that my "playing house" was better than hearing the outright reproach these leaders were bringing to God. In actuality, the difference between me and them was that my sin was (supposedly) done in secret (until I became pregnant which is another story for a later time). To think that I justified my sin, in that I had only one partner, yet I was not married. The sad truth is that sexual perversion (any immoral sex that is contrary to the will of God) is often overlooked and almost accepted in the church. As long as we think that we are fooling others, we think that we were also escaping consequences of sin. Like David, God still wants to use us. The body of Christ has need of your gifts and talents.

Jesus came to save mankind from sins. "He himself bore our sins in his body on the tree, that we might die to sin and live to righteousness. By his wounds you have been healed." (I Peter 2:24)

<u>Words to Chew On:</u> Perhaps being honest with yourself about your relationship with Christ is the first step to having integrity in the rest of your life. The truth is, all of us should be on our way to a burning hell. I've often said that the difference between those in jail who committed a crime is that they got caught. We can be sinking deep in sin all while preaching, singing on the choir, playing instruments and leading for praise and worship, ushering, and serving in ministry, all in the name of the Lord and still miss the mark with our relationship with the Lord. The Word tells us that the wages of sin is death. There may not be an immediate *consequence* to sin, but punishment is certain. David was told by the prophet Nathan what would take place in his family as a direct result of his sin with Bathsheba. Later, we see that David's daughter was raped by her brother and two of David's sons tried to kill David and steal the throne. All of us mess up and fall short of God's glory as Romans 3:23 tells us, but do we continue to stay in bondage or do we break free from a lifestyle of sin? The good news is that while we were in our mess, (While we were yet sinners), Christ died for us. We have hope knowing that, Jesus came so that we may have life

and life abundantly. John 10:10. God desires truth/ integrity in the inner man. Psalm 51:6 "Integrity is doing the right thing, even when no one is watching." Charles Marshall

Prayer: "Have mercy on me, O God,
according to your steadfast love;
according to your abundant mercy
blot out my transgressions.

2 Wash me thoroughly from my iniquity,
and cleanse me from my sin!
3 For I know my transgressions,
and my sin is ever before me.
4 Against you, you only, have I sinned
and done what is evil in your sight,
so that you may be justified in your words
and blameless in your judgment.
5 Behold, I was brought forth in iniquity,
and in sin did my mother conceive me.
6 Behold, you delight in truth in the inward being,
and you teach me wisdom in the secret heart.
7 Purge me with hyssop, and I shall be clean;
wash me, and I shall be whiter than snow.
8 Let me hear joy and gladness;
let the bones that you have broken rejoice.
9 Hide your face from my sins,
and blot out all my iniquities.

10 Create in me a clean heart, O God,
   and renew a right spirit within me.
11 Cast me not away from your presence,
   and take not your Holy Spirit from me.
12 Restore to me the joy of your salvation,
   and uphold me with a willing spirit.
13 Then I will teach transgressors your ways,
   and sinners will return to you.
14 Deliver me from bloodguiltiness, O God,
   O God of my salvation,
   and my tongue will sing aloud of your
   righteousness.
15 O Lord, open my lips,
   and my mouth will declare your praise.
16 For you will not delight in sacrifice, or I
   would give it;
   you will not be pleased with a burnt offering.
17 The sacrifices of God are a broken spirit;
   a broken and contrite heart, O God, you will not
   despise. (Psalm 51:1-17)

Father, I ask for your forgiveness for having a lack of
integrity when it comes to_____. I pray for
pure motifs and a heart of integrity. You told me to
live in the world, but not as the world. (I John 2:15-17)
I repent of _____. *Ask the Holy Spirit to reveal
the spirit you need to renounce: I come against the
spirit of _____ (sexual perversion, lying, manipula-
tion cheating, stealing, gambling, drug use/alcohol,*

covetousness, physical violence, verbal abuse, cursing...etc) Wash me in your blood. Fill me with your Holy Spirit. Thank you for making me clean. In Jesus' name. Amen.

Day 4

REBELLION

Song: "Holy is Our God" By James Fortune

Scripture Reference(s): I Samuel 15:10-31

10 The word of the Lord came to Samuel: 11 "I regret that I have made Saul king, for he has turned back from following me and has not performed my commandments." And Samuel was angry, and he cried to the Lord all night. 12 And Samuel rose early to meet Saul in the morning. And it was told Samuel, "Saul came to Carmel, and behold, he set up a monument for himself and turned and passed on and went down to Gilgal." 13 And Samuel came to Saul, and Saul said to him, "Blessed be you to the Lord. I have performed the commandment of the Lord." 14 And Samuel said, "What then is this bleating of the sheep in my ears and the lowing of the oxen that I hear?" 15 Saul said, "They have brought them from the Amalekites, for the people spared the best of the

sheep and of the oxen to sacrifice to the Lord your God, and the rest we have devoted to destruction." 16 Then Samuel said to Saul, "Stop! I will tell you what the Lord said to me this night." And he said to him, "Speak."

17 And Samuel said, "Though you are little in your own eyes, are you not the head of the tribes of Israel? The Lord anointed you king over Israel. 18 And the Lord sent you on a mission and said, 'Go, devote to destruction the sinners, the Amalekites, and fight against them until they are consumed.' 19 Why then did you not obey the voice of the Lord? Why did you pounce on the spoil and do what was evil in the sight of the Lord?" 20 And Saul said to Samuel, "I have obeyed the voice of the Lord. I have gone on the mission on which the Lord sent me. I have brought Agag the king of Amalek, and I have devoted the Amalekites to destruction. 21 But the people took of the spoil, sheep and oxen, the best of the things devoted to destruction, to sacrifice to the Lord your God in Gilgal." 22 And Samuel said,

"Has the Lord as great delight in burnt offerings and sacrifices,
> as in obeying the voice of the Lord?
Behold, to obey is better than sacrifice,
> and to listen than the fat of rams.
23 For rebellion is as the sin of divination,
> and presumption is as iniquity and idolatry.

Because you have rejected the word of the Lord,
    he has also rejected you from being king."

24 Saul said to Samuel, "I have sinned, for I have transgressed the commandment of the Lord and your words, because I feared the people and obeyed their voice. 25 Now therefore, please pardon my sin and return with me that I may bow before the Lord." 26 And Samuel said to Saul, "I will not return with you. For you have rejected the word of the Lord, and the Lord has rejected you from being king over Israel." 27 As Samuel turned to go away, Saul seized the skirt of his robe, and it tore. 28 And Samuel said to him, "The Lord has torn the kingdom of Israel from you this day and has given it to a neighbor of yours, who is better than you. 29 And also the Glory of Israel will not lie or have regret, for he is not a man, that he should have regret." 30 Then he said, "I have sinned; yet honor me now before the elders of my people and before Israel, and return with me, that I may bow before the Lord your God." 31 So Samuel turned back after Saul, and Saul bowed before the Lord.

Problem In the World: There is a story about a man who was given a few opportunities to be rescued from the receding flood waters in his town. He was stuck on the rooftop of his house as the waters continued to rise. Meanwhile, he prayed to God to help him. A man in a rowboat told him to jump in and he would save him, but the stranded man replied, "No, it's OK, I'm praying to God and he is going to save me." A motorboat came by and said the same thing, but the stranded man said, "No thanks, I'm praying to God and he is going to save me. I have faith." The motorboat went on his way. Next, a helicopter came by and the pilot directed the stranded man to grab hold of the rope so he could be lifted to safety. Again, the stranded man replied, "No thanks, I'm praying to God and he is going to save me. I have faith." Of course, the helicopter flew away. By this time, the water rose above the rooftop and the man drowned. The man died and went to Heaven. The man asked God why God didn't save him. God replied, "I sent you a rowboat and a motorboat and a helicopter, what more did you expect?"

Can you think of a time when you refused godly counsel from a leader or someone well equipped in a specific area whether by personal or professional experience? Instead, when you did not heed the counsel, your plan backfired on you because, "Nobody can tell you what to do because you know everything?" or "You're always right and everybody else is always wrong." Does this sound like you? Do you become defensive when you receive correction? How do you respond when given constructive criticism? The problem is that, "We want what we want and when we want it."

<u>Problem in the Text</u>: Saul was instructed by the Lord through the prophet Samuel to destroy the Amalek people. Instead, Saul speared the life of King Agag. Selective obedience is the same as disobedience. Saul made a conscious decision to do what he wanted to do. His rebellion is likened to iniquity and worshipping idols. Saul's rebellion against the command of the Lord caused him to be rejected as king.

<u>Solution to the text</u>: Saul forfeited his opportunity to be king because of his rebellion. David had no idea that he was going to be anointed as king where the King of all Kings and the Lord of Lords would enter through his bloodline and save the world.

<u>Solution to the World:</u> Many times, God tries to warn us from danger and get our attention from making a costly mistake. However, it seems that we know better than God or those trying to guide us when we rebel against their counsel by doing our own thing. Hebrews 13:17 teaches us to, "Obey those who have rule over you so they may be able to give an account." I can recall countless times that my pastor or husband gave sound direction to me for certain situations that I found myself in. One incident, my husband advised me to put money aside for taxes since I worked as an independent contractor. When the time came to pay taxes, I had to ask my husband for the money. Another incident, my pastor advised me not

to negotiate for more money for a certain job, even though my credentials met the criteria. The offer for employment was rescinded. For some reason, the mindset was, "What are they so worried about? They really don't know what they are talking about. I can do it this way instead and everything will still be fine." Later, I realized after an intense argument with my husband that I was like a little kid who throws a tantrum when things don't go the child's way. Why did I always feel the need to defend my actions when corrected by my pastor? That can only be attributed to stubbornness! Luke 4:18 gives a clear picture why Jesus came:

"The Spirit of the LORD *is* upon Me,
Because He has anointed Me
To preach the gospel to *the* poor;
He has sent Me to heal the brokenhearted,
To proclaim liberty to *the* captives
And recovery of sight to *the* blind,
To set at liberty those who are oppressed;

Words to Chew On: It's plain and simple. [Jesus] He Came to Set the Captives Free!

I Corinthians 11:28, 30-32 says, "But let a man examine himself...For this reason many are weak and sick among you, and many sleep. For if we would judge ourselves, we would not be judged. But when we are judged, we are chastened by the Lord, that we may not be condemned with the world." How have you lived, or how are you living, in rebellion?

Prayer: Holy Spirit, I recognize that I have rebelled against the leadership you have placed over my life. I recognize that it didn't profit me anything but headaches and discord. I'm tired of operating in my own strength and against your will. I ..."cast down arguments and every high thing that exalt itself against the knowledge of God, I bring every thought into captivity to the obedience of Christ." II Corinthians 10:5. I bind up the spirit of rebellion/witchcraft and release the spirit of wisdom and the spirit of obedience. Thank you, Jesus that because of your blood I am set free. In Jesus' Name. Amen

Day 5

COMPLAINING

Song: "The Anthem" Todd Dulaney

Scripture Reference: Ezekiel 37:1-14

The Valley of Dry Bones

37 The hand of the Lord was upon me, and he brought me out in the Spirit of the Lord and set me down in the middle of the valley; it was full of bones. 2 And he led me around among them, and behold, there were very many on the surface of the valley, and behold, they were very dry. 3 And he said to me, "Son of man, can these bones live?" And I answered, "O Lord God, you know." 4 Then he said to me, "Prophesy over these bones, and say to them, O dry bones, hear the word of the Lord. 5 Thus says the Lord God to these bones: Behold, I will cause breath to enter you, and you shall live. 6 And I will lay sinews upon you, and will cause flesh to come upon you, and cover you

with skin, and put breath in you, and you shall live, and you shall know that I am the Lord."

7 So I prophesied as I was commanded. And as I prophesied, there was a sound, and behold, a rattling, and the bones came together, bone to its bone. 8 And I looked, and behold, there were sinews on them, and flesh had come upon them, and skin had covered them. But there was no breath in them. 9 Then he said to me, "Prophesy to the breath; prophesy, son of man, and say to the breath, Thus says the Lord God: Come from the four winds, O breath, and breathe on these slain, that they may live." 10 So I prophesied as he commanded me, and the breath came into them, and they lived and stood on their feet, an exceedingly great army.

11 Then he said to me, "Son of man, these bones are the whole house of Israel. Behold, they say, 'Our bones are dried up, and our hope is lost; we are indeed cut off.' 12 Therefore prophesy, and say to them, Thus says the Lord God: Behold, I will open your graves and raise you from your graves, O my people. And I will bring you into the land of Israel. 13 And you shall know that I am the Lord, when I open your graves, and raise you from your graves, O my people. 14 And I will put my Spirit within you, and you shall live, and I will place you in your own land. Then you shall know that I am the Lord; I have spoken, and I will do it, declares the Lord."

<u>Problem in the World</u>: One morning when my internal alarm clock went off (haven't used an alarm clock since I was a freshman in high school because the Lord proved himself to wake me up at the specific time I ask him) to get up for work, the Holy Spirit convicted me of grumbling and complaining. I started my usual Monday morning off by whining, kicking and screaming about getting out of bed and not wanting to go to work. I mumbled, "God, do I have to go to work...Do I have to deal with that person or will I have to deal with this issue today, and before I knew it, the complaints continued until I heard the Holy Spirit say, "Stop it! Just stop it! Stop complaining! Do everything without grumbling and complaining! Haven't I given you the authority to defeat the powers of darkness and to trample on snakes and scorpions?" (Luke 10:19) He also reminded me of a recent time that I was the substitute teacher for a colleague, and a sticky note lie on her desk, which caught my eye. The sticky note read, "Work is worship." After reading the note, I felt convicted for my complaint about everything concerning work that didn't appear to be going right. I realized how easy it is to pick apart all of the wrong or bad in a situation. Yet, I neglected to focus my attention on what the Word of God says. Suddenly, it was like a bolt of lightning that caused me to sit upright and move swiftly to get dressed. On that very same morning that I went into work, I sprayed water from a spray bottle into the

atmosphere of my work area, prayed and pleaded the Blood of Jesus. The first person who entered the room, stood motionless. He surveyed the room and began to sniff the air like a bloodhound. Still standing, he slowly let out a suspicious, "There's something different in here [the room]." Everything was in place as it had been before. It was the sweet aroma of the Holy Spirit and the power of His Blood. Have you ever been around people who complain about everything? You ask them, "How are you?" and then they make you feel sorry that you asked because they tell you all that's going on in the news or they may say the words of an inaccurate gospel song, "I'm climbing up the rough side of the mountain," Who wants to be around a complaining spirit? That type of negative energy is toxic.

Problem in the Text: Israel was in a state of rebellion where God had to remove himself from them and allow them to hit rock bottom and even die because of their iniquity. They were divided into two nations, Israel and Judah. The Israelites were captives in a foreign land because of God's judgment against them. The bones in the valley represented a spiritual and physical death in that the Israelites had been separated from God and their land for so long. It seemed as if unification and restoration were impossible. They lost their identity being in a foreign land because they were subjected to the laws and customs of the Babylonians. The Israelites were hopeless. God asked Ezekiel, "Can these bones live?". God had just told Ezekiel to prophecy that Israel would be restored.

Solution to the Text: Even though the children of Israel forgot how the Lord delivered them from Egypt and how the Lord miraculously provided food and water for them, the Israelites were a stubborn people who "played the harlot" (Hosea 4:15). Despite error of their ways, the Lord in His infinite mercy, still, demonstrated His love to the Israelites by sharing plans and direction for them. The Lord still told the Israelites that He would bring deliverance and an inheritance to them. He just required that the Israelites honor Him by sanctifying themselves.

Solution to the World: Like the Israelites, many of us have lost hope concerning our situations. "Death and life are in the power of the tongue..." (Proverbs 18:21). We have won the victory through Christ's death. The resurrection power of Jesus Christ came to give us hope. Turn your complaint into thanks and break out in a praise. Every day is a day of thanksgiving! "In everything give thanks for this is the will of God concerning you." (I Thessalonians 5:18). God has given us the same power to speak life into the dry places of our lives. Jesus gave us the power to speak to any mountain, and in His name it shall be done whatsoever we ask in His name. (Mark 11:23) As long as we have breath in our bodies, we are going to go through some things. We are not exempt from life's challenges. II Corinthians 4:7 tells us that we are hard pressed on every side...The problem is not what we go through, the problem lies in how we respond.

Words to Chew On: Activate the power that lies in you. "He has given us authority to trample on snakes and scorpions." (Luke 10:19) People have the tendency to see a glass as half empty instead of half full. Proverbs 18:21 Speak life into your situation. Prophecy to your marriage, prophecy over your children, prophecy over your health, prophecy over your finances, prophecy over your ministry, prophecy over your business, prophecy over your life. Our situation doesn't have to go the way the enemy says it should go. We walk by faith and not by sight. II Corinthians 5:7

Colossians 3:23 says, work as if working for the Lord and not man. Psalm 42:11 admonishes to hope in God and not be so downcast in our soul.

Prayer: Father, I recognize that I have a complaining spirit and haven't been effective with providing solutions. I repent for murmuring and complaining. Help me to speak life into my situation. Forgive me for complaining; I declare those things that are not as though they already are. Romans 4:17. I renounce all lies spoken about my destiny, and my assignment. Help me to remember that," with man it's impossible, but with God all things are possible." Please, block my ears from untruths and increase my faith. You said, if I have faith as a mustard seed I can say to the mountain be removed and it will." Thank you, Jesus, for giving me fresh insight. In Your Name. Amen.

Day 6

SPIRIT OF OFFENSE

Song: "There is Power in the Name of Jesus" Tasha Cobbs

Scripture Reference(s): Genesis 37:12-36; 45:1-15

Joseph Sold by His Brothers

12 Now his brothers went to pasture their father's flock near Shechem. 13 And Israel said to Joseph, "Are not your brothers pasturing the flock at Shechem? Come, I will send you to them." And he said to him, "Here I am." 14 So he said to him, "Go now, see if it is well with your brothers and with the flock, and bring me word." So he sent him from the Valley of Hebron, and he came to Shechem. 15 And a man found him wandering in the fields. And the man asked him, "What are you seeking?" 16 "I am seeking my brothers," he said. "Tell me, please, where they are pasturing the flock." 17 And the man said, "They have gone

away, for I heard them say, 'Let us go to Dothan.'"
So Joseph went after his brothers and found them
at Dothan.
18 They saw him from afar, and before he came near
to them they conspired against him to kill him. 19
They said to one another, "Here comes this dreamer.
20 Come now, let us kill him and throw him into one
of the pits. Then we will say that a fierce animal has
devoured him, and we will see what will become
of his dreams." 21 But when Reuben heard it, he
rescued him out of their hands, saying, "Let us not
take his life." 22 And Reuben said to them, "Shed no
blood; throw him into this pit here in the wilderness,
but do not lay a hand on him"—that he might rescue
him out of their hand to restore him to his father. 23
So when Joseph came to his brothers, they stripped
him of his robe, the robe of many colors that he wore.
24 And they took him and threw him into a pit. The
pit was empty; there was no water in it.
25 Then they sat down to eat. And looking up they
saw a caravan of Ishmaelites coming from Gilead,
with their camels bearing gum, balm, and myrrh, on
their way to carry it down to Egypt. 26 Then Judah
said to his brothers, "What profit is it if we kill our
brother and conceal his blood? 27 Come, let us sell
him to the Ishmaelites, and let not our hand be upon
him, for he is our brother, our own flesh." And his
brothers listened to him. 28 Then Midianite traders
passed by. And they drew Joseph up and lifted him

out of the pit, and sold him to the Ishmaelites for twenty shekels of silver. They took Joseph to Egypt. 29 When Reuben returned to the pit and saw that Joseph was not in the pit, he tore his clothes 30 and returned to his brothers and said, "The boy is gone, and I, where shall I go?" 31 Then they took Joseph's robe and slaughtered a goat and dipped the robe in the blood. 32 And they sent the robe of many colors and brought it to their father and said, "This we have found; please identify whether it is your son's robe or not." 33 And he identified it and said, "It is my son's robe. A fierce animal has devoured him. Joseph is without doubt torn to pieces." 34 Then Jacob tore his garments and put sackcloth on his loins and mourned for his son many days. 35 All his sons and all his daughters rose up to comfort him, but he refused to be comforted and said, "No, I shall go down to Sheol to my son, mourning." Thus his father wept for him. 36 Meanwhile the Midianites had sold him in Egypt to Potiphar, an officer of Pharaoh, the captain of the guard.

Then Joseph could not control himself before all those who stood by him. He cried, "Make everyone go out from me." So no one stayed with him when Joseph made himself known to his brothers. 2 And he wept aloud, so that the Egyptians heard it, and the household of Pharaoh heard it. 3 And Joseph said to his brothers, "I am Joseph! Is my father still alive?"

But his brothers could not answer him, for they were dismayed at his presence.

4 So Joseph said to his brothers, "Come near to me, please." And they came near. And he said, "I am your brother, Joseph, whom you sold into Egypt. 5 And now do not be distressed or angry with yourselves because you sold me here, for God sent me before you to preserve life. 6 For the famine has been in the land these two years, and there are yet five years in which there will be neither plowing nor harvest. 7 And God sent me before you to preserve for you a remnant on earth, and to keep alive for you many survivors. 8 So it was not you who sent me here, but God. He has made me a father to Pharaoh, and lord of all his house and ruler over all the land of Egypt. 9 Hurry and go up to my father and say to him, 'Thus says your son Joseph, God has made me lord of all Egypt. Come down to me; do not tarry. 10 You shall dwell in the land of Goshen, and you shall be near me, you and your children and your children's children, and your flocks, your herds, and all that you have. 11 There I will provide for you, for there are yet five years of famine to come, so that you and your household, and all that you have, do not come to poverty.' 12 And now your eyes see, and the eyes of my brother Benjamin see, that it is my mouth that speaks to you. 13 You must tell my father of all my honor in Egypt, and of all that you have seen. Hurry and bring my

father down here." 14 Then he fell upon his brother Benjamin's neck and wept, and Benjamin wept upon his neck. 15 And he kissed all his brothers and wept upon them. After that his brothers talked with him.

<u>Problem In the World</u>: Many of us are guilty of offending others whether knowingly or unknowingly. For years, people have not spoken to each other because of something that was said or done. Have you ever stopped to ask yourself, "Did *I* say anything wrong to the person that would cause them not even to speak to me? How was my tone when I responded? We are quick to say how others have wronged us, yet, we are slow to look in the mirror at our own actions. As I mentioned in a previous chapter, I was in a relationship prior to becoming married. After the pregnancy didn't go well, the relationship ended abruptly, against my will. I just knew the relationship was headed for marriage. At the time that I was "dumped" I also was told that there was someone else in the picture and the two were also living together. Jealousy and rage filled my heart because the other person clearly enjoyed the niceties that I didn't get to experience. The feeling of betrayal and hurt lasted over a year after that relationship ended. Later, upon becoming involved in another relationship and having an argument, my flaws were pointed out. During the argument, a reference was made to my previous broken relationship in that I was

the one who probably drove that relationship to an end. Wow! That was a hard pill to swallow from my, now husband.

Problem in the Text: Joseph was sold into slavery by his brothers. The plan was to leave Joseph for dead in a pit, until one of the brothers convinced the others not to kill Joseph, rather sell him into slavery. Joseph's brothers brought an offense to Joseph, and their father when they lied about what had happened to Joseph, all without showing any remorse or conscious at that time. Their offense was a transgression against God, their parents, and to Joseph. Years went by and the brothers had not seen or spoken with Joseph. Little did the brothers know that the Lord had elevated Joseph to a Pharoah-like position. While, there was a famine in their land, the brothers unknowingly) came to Joseph for food. Joseph became sorrowful as he recognized his brothers, yet his brothers had not recognized him.

Solution to the Text: Joseph could have remained in a state of bitterness and unforgiveness, but he showed mercy to his brothers and their families. The brothers intended to harm Joseph, but God used it for good. He Joseph to save his people from starving to death." The pain and suffering that Christ endured for us, was meant to kill him. Christ shows his grace toward us, in that while we were yet sinners He died for us. Romans 5:8

Solution to the World: The people who nailed Jesus to the cross, hurled insults at him, spit in his face, and whipped him, greatly offended the King of Kings and the Lord of Lords. Yet, Jesus was the propitiation for our sins and all of our offenses. [Christ's grace is sufficient for us!.] Jesus came to earth and provided a way for us to confess our sins one to another and to repent for the remission of sins John 24:47

Words to Chew On: The spirit of offense that we cause on others evoke all types of ill emotions in them…

The spirit of offense causes one to lose hope and to not believe that they have purpose. On the other hand, we bring a curse on ourselves when we do not repent and seek forgiveness There are three areas that we can offend in: 1.*God*-are you mad at God or blame God for a situation that occurred in life? 2. *People*-do you think that everything people say and do is directly against you? Has someone wronged you by violating your trust? 3.*Yourself*-Do you know who you are and whose you are? Do you find your-self feeling guilty and shameful for a period of time? Do you try to be someone else other than yourself?

<u>Prayer:</u> Father, search my heart and see if there be any offensive way in me. Psalm 139:23-24. Help me to be more like you. Help me to be quick to say, "I am sorry" when I have wronged someone or others. Father, help me to examine myself daily. Break the chains of darkness and offense in me. Thank you that Your lovingkindness is better than life. Psalm 63:3

Day 7

ANGER

<u>Song:</u> "I Worship You in the Spirit" Shekinah Glory

<u>Scripture Reference (s):</u> Genesis 4:1-16

Cain and Abel

1 Now Adam knew Eve his wife, and she conceived and bore Cain, saying, "I have gotten a man with the help of the Lord." 2 And again, she bore his brother Abel. Now Abel was a keeper of sheep, and Cain a worker of the ground. 3 In the course of time Cain brought to the Lord an offering of the fruit of the ground, 4 and Abel also brought of the firstborn of his flock and of their fat portions. And the Lord had regard for Abel and his offering, 5 but for Cain and his offering he had no regard. So Cain was very angry, and his face fell. 6 The Lord said to Cain, "Why are you angry, and why has your face fallen? 7 If you do well, will you not be accepted? And if you do not do

well, sin is crouching at the door. Its desire is contrary to you, but you must rule over it."

8 Cain spoke to Abel his brother. And when they were in the field, Cain rose up against his brother Abel and killed him. 9 Then the Lord said to Cain, "Where is Abel your brother?" He said, "I do not know; am I my brother's keeper?" 10 And the Lord said, "What have you done? The voice of your brother's blood is crying to me from the ground. 11 And now you are cursed from the ground, which has opened its mouth to receive your brother's blood from your hand. 12 When you work the ground, it shall no longer yield to you its strength. You shall be a fugitive and a wanderer on the earth." 13 Cain said to the Lord, "My punishment is greater than I can bear. 14 Behold, you have driven me today away from the ground, and from your face I shall be hidden. I shall be a fugitive and a wanderer on the earth, and whoever finds me will kill me." 15 Then the Lord said to him, "Not so! If anyone kills Cain, vengeance shall be taken on him sevenfold." And the Lord put a mark on Cain, lest any who found him should attack him. 16 Then Cain went away from the presence of the Lord and settled in the land of Nod, east of Eden.

Problem in the World: Feelings of rage and hatred built up in the body becomes toxic. Anger has many effects on our body both physically and emotionally. Health editor, Ryan Jaslow from CBS News wrote an article about a study of anger. He said that anger outbursts are likely to cause heart attacks or strokes within two hours. Anger perpetuates the spirit of murder and suicide—just look at the news or think about what people have done in road rage, disciplining children and more. After that ungodly relationship ended that I mentioned earlier, I recall having fits of anger for several months. Many nights I tossed and turned in bed, thinking how to end the young man's life or mine, but quickly retreated as I considered the consequences or the drastic measures. When I awakened after finally going to sleep, I woke up yelling at God as though He was the blame for my discontented feelings. I wanted to shun away from the church, but I knew that was the safest place for me in that frame of mind. I would sit in church filled with rage as my mind wandered to the place of hurt. The preacher and the choir were drowned out; they sounded like the Charlie Brown movie, "wump wump, wump" where Charlie Brown didn't talk.

<u>Problem in the Text</u>: Cain and Abel were brothers from the first man and woman on earth (Adam and Eve) Cain was a farmer and Abel was a shepherd. Both brought sacrifices to God. However, Cain's offering did not please God, whereas Abel's offering was accepted. Cain became angry and jealous to the point, he took his brother's life.

<u>Solution to the Text</u>: The Lord gave Cain an opportunity to do his sacrifice over. This shows God's tender mercy toward Cain even when messed up.

<u>Solution to the World:</u> Christ sacrificed His blood for us to have access to him in prayer, and for the forgiveness of sins. "How great is the love the father has lavished on us, that we should be called children of God." I John 3:1 and great is His mercy toward us.

When Christ was crucified we were crucified with Him, says the scripture in I Corinthians 1:30. We are admonished to,

<u>Words to Chew On:</u> Anger is like an explosive volcano that spews hot lava and hardens rock. Anger hardens our heart and love can't shine through. There are two types of anger: 1) Righteous and 2) Sinful Anger. Righteous anger is the evil or sin that Christians should hate such as racism, child pornography, slavery and other evils contrary to the Word of the Lord. Righteous anger should cause Christians to seek redemptive action. Sinful anger causes one to harm or want to harm or destroy relationships. Sinful anger causes hurt or even death to others when we say things out of our mouths or operate in destruction that destroys relationships. There are healthy ways to deal with anger. Anger boils down to "self"

when we don't get our way and it shows in the form of tantrums.

Ephesians 6:26-32 tells us to, "Be angry and do not sin; do not let the sun go down on your anger and give no opportunity to the devil. Let the thief no longer steal, but rather let him labor, doing honest work with his own hands, so that he may have something to share with anyone in need. Let no corrupting talk come out of your mouths, but only such as is good for building up, as fits the occasion, that it may give grace to those who hear. And do not grieve the Holy Spirit of God, by whom you were sealed for the day of redemption. "Let all bitterness, wrath, anger and evil speaking be put away from you. Be kind to one another, tenderhearted, forgiving one another, as God in Christ forgave you." Ephesians 4:31 Is anger and bitterness keeping you from pleasing the Lord?.

Prayer: (Anoint yourself and lay your hand on yourself) Father, I recognize that I have an unrighteous spirit of anger in me. Remove the anger and bitterness that is putrefying my soul and clouding my judgment. I bind the spirit of anger. I command the spirit of anger to leave in Jesus' name. My mind is free from accusations and unforgiveness. I lose the spirit of love and the peace of God that surpasses all understanding. Father, you take control over my thoughts. You said that vengeance is yours and you are the one who repays. (Romans 12:19). May you increase and allow me to decrease. Fill me with your Holy Spirit. Help me to allow patience to have its perfect work in me. Not my will, but yours be done. Thank you, Lord for delivering me from rage. In Jesus' name. Amen.

Day 8

FORGIVENESS

Song: Your Grace and Mercy" Mississippi Mass Choir

Scripture Reference: Matthew 18:21-35

The Parable of the

Unforgiving Servant

21 Then Peter came up and said to him, "Lord, how often will my brother sin against me, and I forgive him? As many as seven times?" 22 Jesus said to him, "I do not say to you seven times, but seventy-seven times.
23 "Therefore the kingdom of heaven may be compared to a king who wished to settle accounts with his servants. 2 When he began to settle, one was brought to him who owed him ten thousand talents.25 And since he could not pay, his master ordered him to be sold, with his wife and children and all that he

had, and payment to be made. 26 So the servant fell on his knees, imploring him, 'Have patience with me, and I will pay you everything.' 27 And out of pity for him, the master of that servant released him and forgave him the debt. 28 But when that same servant went out, he found one of his fellow servants who owed him a hundred denarii, and seizing him, he began to choke him, saying, 'Pay what you owe.' 29 So his fellow servant fell down and pleaded with him, 'Have patience with me, and I will pay you.' 30 He refused and went and put him in prison until he should pay the debt. 31 When his fellow servants saw what had taken place, they were greatly distressed, and they went and reported to their master all that had taken place. 32 Then his master summoned him and said to him, 'You wicked servant! I forgave you all that debt because you pleaded with me. 33 And should not you have had mercy on your fellow servant, as I had mercy on you?' 34 And in anger his master delivered him to the jailers, until he should pay all his debt. 35 So also my heavenly Father will do to every one of you, if you do not forgive your brother from your heart."

Problem in the World: According to research by Dr. Michael Barry, a pastor and the author of the book, The Forgiveness Project Study, a study showed that 61% of cancer patients have some type of unforgiveness in their heart. Of the 61 percent of cancer patients having forgiveness issues, more than half were severe. Unforgiveness is likened to a disease according to medical books. According to an article from the CBN News (The Christian Perspective) forgiveness therapy is now being used to help treat diseases, such as cancer. Unforgiveness stumps our growth. It leads to many physical and emotional symptoms: depression, bitterness, and more.

Dr. Steven Standiford, chief of surgery at the Cancer Treatment Centers of America, said that refusing to forgive makes people sick and keeps them that way.

"It's important to treat emotional wounds or disorders because they really can hinder someone's reactions to the treatments, even someone's willingness to pursue treatment," Standiford explained.

"Harboring these negative emotions, this anger and hatred, creates a state of chronic anxiety," he said.

"Chronic anxiety very predictably produces excess adrenaline and cortisol, which deplete the production of natural killer cells, which is your body's foot soldier in the fight against cancer," he explained.

Sadly, people walk around for years with feelings of unforgiveness towards others. Yet, many walk around carefree (like myself) not even knowing that people have been offended and walking around with unforgiveness. A couple of years had passed after a crisis occurred with one of my friends. One day I gave the family a turkey for Thanksgiving. To my surprise, the mother confessed to being angry with me for steering her adult daughter away from dependency; she smoothed it over by saying that my kind gesture made up for the time she felt angry with me. In the recess of my mind I was trying to trace what in the world she was talking about. I had no idea that anyone was upset with me; not alone my friend's mother (whose house I rarely visited). over something that was said that was innocent. How can we not forgive those we see every day and expect God to forgive us whom we don't see.

Problem in the Text: Peter asked Christ how many times should we forgive those who have wronged us. Jesus said not seven, but seventy times seventy. Jesus then likened the kingdom of heaven to a king who wanted to acquit all of his servants of all their debt. There was one servant who owed a huge debt, so his wife and children were about to be thrown into prison. He begged the king for mercy and his debt was forgiven. The servant than went to another person that owed him money and demanded the person to pay up. In fact, the servant choked the man then threw him into prison.

Solution to the Text: Matthew talks a lot about the authority of Christ to forgive. Acts 4:12 No other power in heaven or on earth given whereby men can be saved.

<u>Solution to the World:</u> God who is rich in mercy love us so much. (Ephesians 2:4). Psalm 103:10 says that God does not deal with us as our sins deserve. The truth of the matter is that everyone should be in jail or on their way to hell.

<u>Words to Chew On:</u> . "How can we say that we love God whom we do not see, and hate our brother whom we do see?" I John 4:20. Barry Standiford said the first step in learning to forgive is to realize how much we have been forgiven by God.

"When a person forgives from the heart which is the gold standard we see in Matthew 18, forgiveness from the heart we find that they are able to find a sense of peacefulness. Quite often our patients refer to that as a feeling of lightness," he said.

Barry said most people don't realize what a burden anger and hatred were until they let them go.

What if God treated us the way we treated others, almost like slamming a sledgehammer on everything others do? What if God was not merciful toward us for every wrong we commit? How can we say that we love God whom we do not see, and hate our brother whom we do see?" I John 4:20

<u>Prayer:</u> Thank you, Father that "[You don't treat me as my sins deserve.]" Psalm 103:10-14. "Father, forgive me for harboring unforgiveness, root it out and

take it out. Place love in my heart because you are love. You said that he that does not love, does not know you." I John 4:7-8. Remember my sins as far as the east is from the west; teach me how to forgive. Psalm 103:12 Father, please help me to forgive _____ for _____ . I want to experience your freedom in my life. I need you to help me to see _____ as you see them. In Jesus' name, I pray. Amen.

(It is recommended to seek individual/group professional therapy for deep wounds.)

Day 9

DESTINY

Song: "I'm On My Way" Anton Milton

Scripture Reference: I Samuel 16:1-13

The Lord said to Samuel, "How long will you grieve over Saul, since I have rejected him from being king over Israel? Fill your horn with oil, and go. I will send you to Jesse the Bethlehemite, for I have provided for myself a king among his sons." 2 And Samuel said, "How can I go? If Saul hears it, he will kill me." And the Lord said, "Take a heifer with you and say, 'I have come to sacrifice to the Lord.' 3 And invite Jesse to the sacrifice, and I will show you what you shall do. And you shall anoint for me him whom I declare to you." 4 Samuel did what the Lord commanded and came to Bethlehem. The elders of the city came to meet him trembling and said, "Do you come peaceably?" 5 And he said, "Peaceably; I have come to sacrifice to the Lord. Consecrate yourselves, and come with me to the sacrifice." And he consecrated Jesse and his sons and invited them to the sacrifice. 6 When they came, he looked on Eliab and thought, "Surely the Lord's anointed is before him." 7 But the Lord said to Samuel, "Do not look on his appearance or on the height of his stature, because I have rejected him. For the Lord sees not as man sees: man looks on the outward appearance, but the Lord looks on the heart." 8 Then Jesse called Abinadab and made him pass before Samuel. And he said, "Neither has the Lord chosen this one." 9 Then Jesse made Shammah pass by. And he said, "Neither has the Lord chosen this one." 10 And Jesse made seven of his sons pass before Samuel. And Samuel said to Jesse, "The Lord has not chosen these." 11 Then Samuel said to Jesse, "Are all your sons here?" And he said, "There remains yet the youngest, but behold, he is keeping the sheep." And Samuel said to Jesse, "Send and get him, for we will not sit down till he comes here." 12 And he sent and brought him in. Now he was ruddy and had beautiful eyes and was handsome. And the Lord said, "Arise, anoint him, for this is he." 13 Then Samuel took the horn of oil and anointed him in the midst of his brothers. And the Spirit of the Lord rushed upon David from that day forward. And Samuel rose up and went to Ramah.

Problem in the World: Many people have been discounted for their inability to fit in like everyone else.

There are celebrities from all walks of life from poet, politician, comedian, singer, to sports figure, who beat the odds of becoming great, not according to man's standard. The odds stacked against them include coming from a family of violence, poverty, alcohol and drug use, or physical disability. Take for instance, Ashley Dudd who became a great actress after being neglected and surrounded by drug use, actor Bruce Willis who overcame stuttering, singer Rihanna who had a violent family history, Olympic skater Kristi Yamaguchi who had a club foot and the list goes on.

People put labels on us before our time; therefore, we operate in a role that is not ours.

Problem in the Text: Samuel was certain that Eliab, one of Jesse's sons, was chosen to be king because of his outward appearance; Jesse's other two sons passed before Samuel but, God rejected them. Instead, David was chosen among his brothers to become king.

Solution to the Text: God told Samuel that he would declare to him who he should anoint, but Samuel immediately saw Eliab and thought he was the one. Although Jesse allowed two of his other sons to pass before Samuel, Samuel knew to wait on God and asked if there were more sons because it didn't line up with what God said: the king would come from Jesse's line.

Solution to the World: Christ came to save the lost not those who are already saved. God has chosen us before the foundation of the world. "Before I formed you in the womb I knew you, and before you were born I consecrated you;

I appointed you a prophet to the nations." Jeremiah 1:5. There will come a time on judgment day that everyone will have to give an account to Christ for every deed and work they've done in these earthly bodies.

Words to Chew On: We must make sure that we are fulfilling our assignment. As early as the second grade, I didn't feel like I fit in with the other children. Perhaps, it was because I gravitated to the "friendless" or people who were made fun of for being different. In second grade, I recall a friend who walked with one leg turned inward. No one wanted to volunteer to walk with her in the hall when she had to run an errand or go to the restroom (two people were required to walk another in the school building), except for me. There was a perception that my friend's disability made her incompetent, which was far from the truth. As a junior missionary visiting the sick and shut in, even at the fourth grade level, I was the child who wanted to hug and pray everyone to good health even if they smelled. By the time I was in the seventh grade, I was called a "nerd" because I excelled in school and played the flute, traveled 45 minutes and arrived to school before all of my friends and teachers had, when no one but the janitors and the music instructor were in school to practice for a competitive band and orchestra. As a minority, excelling academically and musically were frowned upon by my peers; staying after school for track was accepted. Throughout middle school and high school, I thought for sure that I was "ugly" because my female friends and older sister were always asked out by boys. In middle school, I hung around so-called friends just to be in the in crowd and for protection since I and my sister were no longer at the same school. These friends would get poor grades, have boyfriends and display intimate affection on public transportation, wear designer clothes and fresh hairstyles, and fight for each other if necessary. My stomach would cringe at their wrongdoings. I didn't feel comfortable using profanity with my "so called friends." Through maturity, I now know that I was unpopular because of the call God had on my life and I didn't know that I was destined for greatness.

In high school, often I ate alone at lunch and didn't mind it because I didn't want to be a part of the crowd with people sleeping around. I never was one to have a lot of friends, maybe one main friend (who even then didn't have my best interest in mind; the three friends throughout my school years I remember always talked about themselves). At an early age, I was about a kingdom work. While in high school, I founded the outreach ministry for homeless and directed the children's choir at the church my father pastored. After my family and I relocated to Philadelphia from Massachusetts, we moved into the Mount Airy section of Philadelphia, a step up from the Logan section of Philadelphia where I grew up. As a child from the inner city, I remember riding through the nicer neighborhoods wondering if I could one day live there; eventually I went to undergraduate college and didn't have a student loan until my senior year of college which was only like $3,000. (I received scholarships and donations) Perhaps, people have discounted you and may have told you that you wouldn't be anything or that you would (negatively) be just like a family member. What does the Word say about who you are and whose you are? "Before I formed you in the womb I knew you, and before you were born I consecrated you; I appointed you a prophet to the nations." Jeremiah 1:5. You are destined for greatness. God takes the ordinary to do extraordinary things, just like He did when he appointed David to be king.

<u>Prayer:</u> (Lay hands on yourself and pray and decree aloud). Holy Spirit, show me who I am in the Spirit. Help me to declare your Word over my life and to declare who you say that I am. I thank you that, I am the head and not the tail, above and not beneath. (Deuteronomy 28:13) In all these things I am more than a conqueror. (Romans 8:37). Thank you, Father that I am the righteousness of God. (II Corinthians 5:21). Thank you, Lord that I am a royal priesthood, holy and acceptable to you. (I Peter 2:9) Use my circumstances you're your glory. Thank you, Lord, for revealing truth about who you say I am through your Word and through your cleansing blood. Thank you Lord that you've destined me for greatness.

Day 10

WORSHIP

<u>Song:</u> "Consuming Fire" Todd Dulaney"/ "There is Nothing Like the Presence of the Lord" William McDowell

<u>Scripture Reference: </u>Leviticus 10

The Death of Nadab and Abihu

Now Nadab and Abihu, the sons of Aaron, each took his censer and put fire in it and laid incense on it and offered unauthorized fire before the Lord, which he had not commanded them. 2 And fire came out from before the Lord and consumed them, and they died before the Lord. 3 Then Moses said to Aaron, "This is what the Lord has said: 'Among those who are near me I will be sanctified, and before all the people I will be glorified.'" And Aaron held his peace.

4 And Moses called Mishael and Elzaphan, the sons of Uzziel the uncle of Aaron, and said to them, "Come near; carry your brothers away from the front of the sanctuary and out of the camp." 5 So they came near and carried them in their coats out of the camp, as Moses had said. 6 And Moses said to Aaron and to Eleazar and Ithamar his sons, "Do not let the hair of your heads hang loose, and do not tear your clothes, lest you die, and wrath come upon all the congregation; but let your brothers, the whole house of Israel, bewail the burning that the Lord has kindled. 7 And do not go outside the entrance of the tent of meeting, lest you die, for the anointing oil of the Lord is upon you." And they did according to the word of Moses.

8 And the Lord spoke to Aaron, saying, 9 "Drink no wine or strong drink, you or your sons with you, when you go into the tent of meeting, lest you die. It shall be a statute forever throughout your generations. 10 You are to distinguish between the holy and the common, and between the unclean and the clean, 11 and you are to teach the people of Israel all the statutes that the Lord has spoken to them by Moses." 12 Moses spoke to Aaron and to Eleazar and Ithamar, his surviving sons: "Take the grain offering that is left of the Lord's food offerings, and eat it unleavened beside the altar, for it is most holy. 13 You shall eat it in a holy place, because it is your due and your sons' due, from the Lord's food offerings, for so I am commanded. 14 But the breast that is waved and the

thigh that is contributed you shall eat in a clean place, you and your sons and your daughters with you, for they are given as your due and your sons' due from the sacrifices of the peace offerings of the people of Israel. 15 The thigh that is contributed and the breast that is waved they shall bring with the food offerings of the fat pieces to wave for a wave offering before the Lord, and it shall be yours and your sons' with you as a due forever, as the Lord has commanded." 16 Now Moses diligently inquired about the goat of the sin offering, and behold, it was burned up! And he was angry with Eleazar and Ithamar, the surviving sons of Aaron, saying, 17 "Why have you not eaten the sin offering in the place of the sanctuary, since it is a thing most holy and has been given to you that you may bear the iniquity of the congregation, to make atonement for them before the Lord? 18 Behold, its blood was not brought into the inner part of the sanctuary. You certainly ought to have eaten it in the sanctuary, as I commanded." 19 And Aaron said to Moses, "Behold, today they have offered their sin offering and their burnt offering before the Lord, and yet such things as these have happened to me! If I had eaten the sin offering today, would the Lord have approved?" 20 And when Moses heard that, he approved.

Problem in the World: Many Christians have an outward appearance that they are "holy," deep into God or religious law abiding people. They may carry a big Bible to indicate that they read the Bible or have substantial Bible knowledge; they know how to dance and shout with the right music (to be seen by others, but not inspired by the Lord if they are from a Pentecostal denomination); they know how to speak in unknown tongues (so others can hear them); they know how to pray long prayers, using big words; Christians may sing on the choir and wear the best robes; they may serve in the church as an usher, or even preach in the pulpit. Contrary to popular belief that a man who is dressed nicely in a suit or a woman who looks very well polished are "good people and can be trusted" is far from the truth. In my experience, I've seen drug dealers dress professionally or wear a bookbag as if they were enrolled in school. While working at a law firm during my undergraduate college years, I was introduced to a very polished prostitute who was very astute in manipulating the system. How do you appear before the Lord? Does He see a pure heart or form and fashion?

Problem in the Text: Nadab and Abihu were brothers who were training to be priests. There were specific requirements for the priest to enter the Tent of Meeting to go beyond the veil and into the holy of holies. They had to wash in a basin. They had a string attached to them with a cow bell. As long as the people heard the bell, they knew all was well.

Nadab and Abihu offered strange fire before the Lord. Moses had already instructed the people how they should give offering to the Lord. For whatever reason, the brothers gave a profane fire when they came into the presence of the Lord for worship. Some speculate that the Nadab and Abihu were drunk. Perhaps they were drunk; or, did they disregard the holiness of God? Whatever the case, they were killed instantly for dishonoring God in the act of worship.

Solution to the text: The people witnessed firsthand what happens when you show disregard to the holiness of God. Eleazar and. Ithamar, Aaron's remaining sons were afraid to eat the bread that they were required to eat from the altar after seeing their two brothers die. The Lord had Aaron repeat the instructions to the Israelites how they should enter into his presence and present offerings. It didn't matter that Nadab and Abihu were PK's (or pastor's kids).

Solution to the World: Regardless of your family background, social status, where you live or where you are from, your political affiliation, educational background, or all of your accomplishments, Christ came for all; and all must bow before the Almighty Creator, the King of Kings and the Lord of Lords. "Therefore God has highly exalted him and bestowed on him the name that is above every name, 10 so that at the name of Jesus every knee should bow, in heaven and on earth and under the earth, 11 and every tongue confess that Jesus Christ is Lord, to the glory of God the Father shall bow and every tongue must confess that Jesus Christ is Lord." Philippians 2:9-11. Christ came because of the sinful state of man. He wants to redeem man from going to an eternal burning hell. "For all have sinned and fallen short of the glory of God." Romans 3:23. When we sin, Romans 6:23 tells us that "The wages of sin is death, but the gift of God is eternal life." Hebrews 12:29 says, "Our God is a consuming fire." Christ came to burn all of our failures, inadequacies, insufficiencies and all sin.

Words to Chew On: A lot of times we are looking for a move of God in our situations, yet we have not marinated in the presence of the Lord in true worship. When we come into the presence of Almighty God, we must remember that He is holy and there is no other beside Him. "They that worship me must worship me in spirit and in truth." John 4:23-24. There is a consequence for sin. Our sins may not have an immediate consequence; or if the consequence is immediate, it could result in death like Nadab and Abihu. Romans 6:23 The wages of sin is death. Only a holy God can wipe our slate of sin clean. "Thus you are to be holy to Me, for I the LORD am holy; and I have set you apart from the peoples to be Mine. Leviticus 20:26 "You are my witnesses," declares the Lord,

"and my servant whom I have chosen,
that you may know and believe me
        and understand that I am he.
Before me no god was formed,
        nor shall there be any after me.
11 I, I am the Lord,
        and besides me there is no savior."
        Isaiah 43:10

I saw a story the other day with an African actress who was preparing fish for a meal. After the fish was marinated and cooked, the young daughter had a hard time understanding the process that the fish still could not be eaten because there were bones that had to be removed. I want to go on to say that we want God to move but we haven't taken the time to marinate and get into God's presence. Be careful what we allow to come in our temple because it clouds our spiritual judgment. Having a form of godliness but denying the power thereof. II Timothy 3:5-7. Worship is presenting our body as a living sacrifice. The world judges people based on looks and material possession. When it comes to being in the presence of the Lord, we can fool man, not God. God sees all and knows all. "These people draw near with their lips but their heart is far from me." Matthew 15:8-9 Christ said that he would rather us be hot or cold and not lukewarm or he will spew us out of his mouth. Revelation 3:15-17. Many times, our disobedience does not have an immediate consequence and the consequence may manifest later. Sometimes our disobedience will cost us our life as in the case of Nadab and Abihu. What do you need God to burn in you? Is there anything or anyone in your life who has taken the place of the Lord? We must remember that God is a jealous God and we should not have anything or anyone else before him; There is a way that seems right to man but in the end it leads to death. Proverbs 14:12

Prayer: Holy Spirit, thank you that you are a consuming fire, all loving, all knowing, all powerful God. Draw me closer to you. Forgive me for giving you lip service and having a heart that is so far from you. Isaiah 29:13. Restore the joy of my salvation. Psalm 51:12-14. Thank you that you see my heart. Forgive me Lord for not reverencing your holiness and taking heed to godly instruction. Burn everything in me that is not like you, Lord! Not my will, but yours be done! Give me a broken and contrite heart. (Psalm 51:17) May I have a pure worship experience with you.

Day 11

SELFISHNESS

Song: "I Need Your Glory" Ernest Pugh/James Fortune

Scripture Reference: I Kings 21:1-15

Naboth's Vineyard

21 Now Naboth the Jezreelite had a vineyard in Jezreel, beside the palace of Ahab king of Samaria. 2 And after this Ahab said to Naboth, "Give me your vineyard, that I may have it for a vegetable garden, because it is near my house, and I will give you a better vineyard for it; or, if it seems good to you, I will give you its value in money." 3 But Naboth said to Ahab, "The Lord forbid that I should give you the inheritance of my fathers." 4 And Ahab went into his house vexed and sullen because of what Naboth the Jezreelite had said to him, for he had said, "I will not give you the inheritance of my fathers." And he lay

down on his bed and turned away his face and would eat no food.

5 But Jezebel his wife came to him and said to him, "Why is your spirit so vexed that you eat no food?" 6 And he said to her, "Because I spoke to Naboth the Jezreelite and said to him, 'Give me your vineyard for money, or else, if it please you, I will give you another vineyard for it.' And he answered, 'I will not give you my vineyard.'" 7 And Jezebel his wife said to him, "Do you now govern Israel? Arise and eat bread and let your heart be cheerful; I will give you the vineyard of Naboth the Jezreelite."

8 So she wrote letters in Ahab's name and sealed them with his seal, and she sent the letters to the elders and the leaders who lived with Naboth in his city. 9 And she wrote in the letters, "Proclaim a fast, and set Naboth at the head of the people. 10 And set two worthless men opposite him, and let them bring a charge against him, saying, 'You have cursed God and the king.' Then take him out and stone him to death." 11 And the men of his city, the elders and the leaders who lived in his city, did as Jezebel had sent word to them. As it was written in the letters that she had sent to them, 12 they proclaimed a fast and set Naboth at the head of the people. 13 And the two worthless men came in and sat opposite him. And the worthless men brought a charge against Naboth in the presence of the people, saying, "Naboth cursed God and the king." So they took him outside the city

and stoned him to death with stones. 14 Then they sent to Jezebel, saying, "Naboth has been stoned; he is dead."

15 As soon as Jezebel heard that Naboth had been stoned and was dead, Jezebel said to Ahab, "Arise, take possession of the vineyard of Naboth the Jezreelite, which he refused to give you for money, for Naboth is not alive, but dead." 16 And as soon as Ahab heard that Naboth was dead, Ahab arose to go down to the vineyard of Naboth the Jezreelite, to take possession of it.

Problem in the World: People want more power, more money, more recognition, and more material possessions. They can't seem to have enough and they will do almost anything to attain it: murder, lie, steal, have ungodly sex and relationships, and more. In the Netflix television series House of Cards, the show portrays ruthless politicians who will do any-thing to have power; it doesn't matter who they have to step over or who they have to kill, or relationships they have to severe, as long as they get what they want. Namely, actor Kevin Spacey who plays the character Blair Underwood as both Congressman and President of the United States was vicious in invoking fear in the American people for his gain.

Problem in the Text: Naboth was a righteous man and had land that he inherited through the family. King

Ahab asked for the land several times, but Naboth wouldn't budge and said I cannot sell my inheritance. King Ahab goes home pouting and Jezebel inquired of his disposition. She told him he was the king. She then goes behind his back to hire two scoundrels to lie against Naboth so that Ahab would get the land. Ahab pouted and sulked, so Jezebel had Naboth killed in Ahab's name. Ahab didn't show any remorse for Naboth or his family.

Solution to the Text: Ahab could have repented and humbled himself when he was confronted by the prophet. God hates sin! Ahab caused Israel to sin. In the book of Exodus, God told Moses, "I am the Lord God. I am merciful and very patient with My people. I show great love, and I can be trusted. I keep My promises to My people forever, but I also punish anyone who sins." Exodus 34:7. Ahab and Jezebel thought they gained the entire world through greed. The Lord sent his wrath and had them killed through a dishonorable death where dogs and birds ate their flesh and everyone who belonged to Ahab.

Solution to the World: "Behold, the Lord's hand is not shortened, that it cannot save; nor His ear heavy, that it cannot hear. But your iniquities have separated you from your God; And your sins have hidden His face from you, so that He will not hear." Isaiah 59:1 Jesus can make you whole. Psalm 103 talks about the God who can blot out your transgressions as though they never happened, who can heal all diseases, who can make the lame walk, and the blind to see. Jesus said, Behold, I stand at the door and knock if any man hears my voice and opens the door I will come in and sup with him and he with me. John 3:16 says, "For God so loved the world that He gave His only begotten Son for you and for me. That whosoever believes in Him should not perish but have everlasting life."

Words to Chew On: Do you live for self or do you live wholeheartedly for God? Is your life filled with seeking fame and fortune? We live in a society where people like to gratify self. People are always seeking self -promotion and power. In seeking to please self, many have the attitude, "I don't care who is affected by what I say or do or how I do it, as long as I get mine." When there are worship services held in the church, are lives being changed or is it just another purposeless service that glorify man? Many people have a sense of entitlement. The world and everybody owes them something. How many people have you helped or sought to make a difference in their life, lately? When was the last time you did a kind deed or said a kind word to someone? What does it profit a man to gain the whole world and lose his soul "do nothing from selfishness or empty conceit, but with humility of mind regard one another as more important than yourselves; do not merely look out for your own personal interests, but also for the interests of others" Philippians 2:3-4 "Then Jesus said to His disciples, 'If anyone desires to come after Me, let him deny himself, and take up his cross, and follow Me. For whoever desires to save his life will lose it, but whoever loses his life for My sake will find it.'" Matthew 16:24-25

Prayer: My God! Please show me the area in my life that you need me act in faith and to walk in freedom. Almighty Father, I confess and by an act of my will I repent in Jesus name for being consumed with greed. I command every spirit of greed, insecurity, and fear, to go in the name of Jesus. Teach me how to walk in the Spirit so I will not fulfill the lust of the flesh. (Galatians 5:16-17)

Day 12

GREED

<u>Song:</u> "Trust In You" Anthony Brown and Group Therapy

<u>Scripture Reference</u>: II Kings 5:15-27

15 Then he returned to the man of God, he and all his company, and he came and stood before him. And he said, "Behold, I know that there is no God in all the earth but in Israel; so accept now a present from your servant." 16 But he said, "As the Lord lives, before whom I stand, I will receive none." And he urged him to take it, but he refused. 17 Then Naaman said, "If not, please let there be given to your servant two mule loads of earth, for from now on your servant will not offer burnt offering or sacrifice to any god but the Lord. 18 In this matter may the Lord pardon your servant: when my master goes into the house of Rimmon to worship there, leaning on my arm, and I bow myself in the house of Rimmon, when I bow

myself in the house of Rimmon, the Lord pardon your servant in this matter." 19 He said to him, "Go in peace."

But when Naaman had gone from him a short distance, 20 Gehazi, the servant of Elisha the man of God, said, "See, my master has spared this Naaman the Syrian, in not accepting from his hand what he brought. As the Lord lives, I will run after him and get something from him." 21 So Gehazi followed Naaman. And when Naaman saw someone running after him, he got down from the chariot to meet him and said, "Is all well?" 22 And he said, "All is well. My master has sent me to say, 'There have just now come to me from the hill country of Ephraim two young men of the sons of the prophets. Please give them a talent of silver and two changes of clothing.'" 23 And Naaman said, "Be pleased to accept two talents." And he urged him and tied up two talents of silver in two bags, with two changes of clothing, and laid them on two of his servants. And they carried them before Gehazi. 24 And when he came to the hill, he took them from their hand and put them in the house, and he sent the men away, and they departed. 25 He went in and stood before his master, and Elisha said to him, "Where have you been, Gehazi?" And he said, "Your servant went nowhere." 26 But he said to him, "Did not my heart go when the man turned from his chariot to meet you? Was it a time to accept money and garments, olive orchards and vineyards, sheep and oxen, male servants and female servants? 27 Therefore the leprosy of Naaman shall cling to you and to your descendants forever." So he went out from his presence a leper, like snow.

Problem in the World: Have you ever seen the show or heard of the show called Hoarders? It's a series of TV episodes that capture the lives of people who hoard all types of material things and some hoard animals to the point that to those looking in it looks like clutter, but to them it is normal.

In this show, professional psychiatrists and orga-nizers work together on each of the cases to attempt to bring back some kind of order to the chaotic lives of the individuals being profiled. Typical episodes may show a house covered in animal and human feces; refrigerators full of food more than a year old, clothing and other objects piled up to the ceiling. Roach and rodent infestations are highly common in these hoarding situations. The rooms in the home lose their function completely. From bathrooms no longer functioning and become storage rooms to kitchens becoming virtual cat litter boxes. It reminds me of my former landlord's apartment. She was up in years with a strong personality. Papers covered what may have been a couch, unwashed dishes from days or years, bathroom couldn't walk in, all types of newspapers and papers on the table. It was a place where you didn't want to sit down or use the bathroom because you would step on something. When she passed, my husband and I were asked if we wanted to move downstairs so that we would have access to the basement with our first child. We moved downstairs with strict stipulations of the carpet being removed. We were able to enjoy the natural beauty of the apartment such as seeing the brand new walls, wooden floors, and the greenhouse the landlord already had in place. As Christians, many have lost focus on the One who is our provider and way maker because we are trying to obtain more material possessions. Many are not good stewards over the resources the Lord has already given us.

Problem in the Text: Elisha vowed that he would not take any money or clothing or anything from the hand of Naaman who was sent by the Syrian king to be healed of his leprosy. The Syrians kidnapped a girl from Israel who told Naaman's wife that there was a prophet in the land of Israel who could heal Naaman. Elisha told Naaman to wash in the river seven times, but Naaman thought he should be in two other rivers that the Israelites didn't use. Once he listened to his servants and saw that his skin was new like a baby, he offered gifts to Elisha. Elisha refused. Elisha's servant wanted the material possessions supplied by the Syrian king. The servant was present and heard Elisha's and Naaman's conversation. Perhaps he feared not having enough or he wanted to feel empowered. He forgot the miraculous signs that Elisha performed through the power of God. He forgot that the same God who supplied his master's needs and his needs before was the same God who would supply their needs again. In order to attain wealth, he lied to Naaman and he lied to Elisha when Elisha asked him where he was. His greed caused him and his family to become leprous like Naaman.

Solution to the Text: Gehazi's spiritual leader was so in tune with the Lord that Elisha's spirit went with him when Gehazi secretly went after Naaman. Elisha was training Gehazi how to do what he does.

Solution to the World: Greed is usually associated with lying and or deception and murder. People will do almost anything to obtain more without thinking of people who will be affected. Jesus hung on the cross between two thieves whether the thieves needed more to survive or whether they were seeking riches. Christ loved us so deeply that he took a stripe for the sins and lusts of the flesh that Galatians 5:19-26 talks about.

He took a stripe for greed; he took a stripe for adultery; he took a stripe for fornication; he took a stripe for sexual immorality; he took a stripe for stealing; he took a stripe for misuse of position; he took a stripe for our wild and out of control partying behavior; he took a stripe for our stubbornness; he took a stripe for every idol we've put before God, He took a stripe for hatred, discord, jealousy, fits of rage, selfish ambition, dissensions, and envy; drunkenness, orgies, he took a stripe for every sinful act.

People constantly change; they say one thing today and do another the next day. A person I've known for years, criticized others for their involvement in "playing numbers" with gambling. Before I knew it, the person became obsessed with playing scratch off cards, and "playing numbers." The person didn't realize that they came to rely on playing numbers as their source and was getting deeper into debt. "Jesus came that we may have life and have it more abundantly". John 10:10. "God does not change. He is the same yesterday, today and forevermore." Malachi 3:6

Words to Chew On: What does it profit a man to gain the whole world...for where your treasure is there your heart will be also. "Cast your cares on God for he cares for you." I Peter 5:7

Prayer: Father, forgive me for not trusting you to supply all of my needs. (Philippians 4:19) Help me to seek first the kingdom of God and your righteousness and all these things will be added unto me (Matthew 6:33). Father, help to delight myself in you and you will grant me the desires of your heart. Take greed away from me. I yield to your Holy Spirit. Thank you for teaching me how to trust you with all of my heart, mind, and soul.

Day 13

SPIRITUAL DULLNESS

<u>Song:</u> "Open My Eyes Lord" Maranatha Singers

<u>Scripture Reference:</u> II Kings 6:8-23

Horses and Chariots of Fire

8 Once when the king of Syria was warring against Israel, he took counsel with his servants, saying, "At such and such a place shall be my camp." 9 But the man of God sent word to the king of Israel, "Beware that you do not pass this place, for the Syrians are going down there." 10 And the king of Israel sent to the place about which the man of God told him. Thus he used to warn him, so that he saved himself there more than once or twice.

11 And the mind of the king of Syria was greatly troubled because of this thing, and he called his servants and said to them, "Will you not show me who of us is for the king of Israel?" 12 And one of his servants

said, "None, my lord, O king; but Elisha, the prophet who is in Israel, tells the king of Israel the words that you speak in your bedroom." 13 And he said, "Go and see where he is, that I may send and seize him." It was told him, "Behold, he is in Dothan." 14 So he sent there horses and chariots and a great army, and they came by night and surrounded the city.

15 When the servant of the man of God rose early in the morning and went out, behold, an army with horses and chariots was all around the city. And the servant said, "Alas, my master! What shall we do?" 16 He said, "Do not be afraid, for those who are with us are more than those who are with them." 17 Then Elisha prayed and said, "O Lord, please open his eyes that he may see." So the Lord opened the eyes of the young man, and he saw, and behold, the mountain was full of horses and chariots of fire all around Elisha. 18 And when the Syrians came down against him, Elisha prayed to the Lord and said, "Please strike this people with blindness." So he struck them with blindness in accordance with the prayer of Elisha. 19 And Elisha said to them, "This is not the way, and this is not the city. Follow me, and I will bring you to the man whom you seek." And he led them to Samaria.

20 As soon as they entered Samaria, Elisha said, "O Lord, open the eyes of these men, that they may see." So the Lord opened their eyes and they saw, and behold, they were in the midst of Samaria. 21 As

soon as the king of Israel saw them, he said to Elisha, "My father, shall I strike them down? Shall I strike them down?" 22 He answered, "You shall not strike them down. Would you strike down those whom you have taken captive with your sword and with your bow? Set bread and water before them, that they may eat and drink and go to their master." 23 So he prepared for them a great feast, and when they had eaten and drunk, he sent them away, and they went to their master. And the Syrians did not come again on raids into the land of Israel.

Problem in the World: There is something seriously wrong when Christians can live in the world and as the world does without any conviction or remorse. I've known professing Christians who have convinced themselves that it is okay to live with an unmarried partner, go to the bar or consume excessive alcohol and alter their state of mind (in which they've become drunken), men in leadership who verbally and physically abuse their wives all while serving in ministry in the name of the Lord. What are your motifs for doing "the work of the Lord"?

Is it to be seen by men or is it a selfless act? Do we go to church to really meet God or do we go as a social club or to appear holy? What is your prayer time or personal relationship with the Lord like? Is it out of a sense of duty or are you really expecting to

commune with the Lord as a conscious need or to fulfill a religious act like legalism? Christians live in the
world and try to live as the world does, but scripture
tells us, "not to be conformed to this world but to be
transformed by the renewing of our mind." Romans
12:2 Our natural and spiritual senses are dull; When
we engage in a lifestyle of sin, it brings on God's
wrath and judgment.

A lot of times as believers we are not able to experience the pure worship of God because those things
keep us from inheriting the kingdom of God. "Now
the works of the flesh are evident, which are: adultery, fornication, uncleanness, licentiousness, idolatry, sorcery, . . . of which I tell you beforehand, just
as I also told you in time past, that those who practice such things will not inherit the kingdom of God.
(Galatians 5:19-21)

Problem in the Text:
The Syrian king wanted to attack the Israelites but
every time he planned to do so, his plans were
thwarted and he was unable to carry them out. He
thought there was a leak with his servants so he
called them all to him and asked them if they were
for him or the Israelite king. The servants told the
king they were for him, but that there was a man who
speaks every word he says. God told Elisha the very
plans of the king so that he could alert the Israelite
king. The Syrian king sent soldiers with horses and

chariots after Elisha because Elisha knew of and told the Israelite king of the plans of the Syrian king to attack. They surrounded Elisha, and his servant became afraid because he was seeing through his natural eye. It is possible that the servant was busy serving the man of God that he didn't build his relationship with the Lord through prayer in that he relied on his flesh to make decisions.

Solution to the Text: The king of Israel was sensitive to the voice of the Lord through the prophet who was warned of impending attacks and harm for the Israelites.. Elisha asked the Lord to open the servant's eyes so that the servant could see in the spirit. Although in the natural they were surrounded by an army of men, when the servant's spiritual eyes were opened, he was able to see the angels with chariots of fire surrounding them. On the other hand, Elisha asked the Lord to blind the Syrian army. God is merciful, when Elisha led the Syrian army to Samaria he could have commanded the Israelite army to kill the Syrians; he even gave them food and water, all for the glory of the Lord. For a long while, the Syrians didn't raid the Israelites.

Solution to the World: Even in our messed up sinful state, when our spiritual sight is clouded by sin, God still loves us. (It's not a ticket to continue in sin) "Who shall separate us from the love of Christ?

Shall trouble or hardship or persecution or famine or nakedness or danger or sword?" Romans 8:35. We must remember that one day we will give an account for what we've done in our earthly bodies and we shall see Christ face to face. Revelation 1:7 prophesies: "Behold, He is coming with clouds, and every eye will see Him, even they also who pierced Him. And all the tribes of earth will mourn because of Him." They will see Him as Judge. Revelation 22:4 says of those who will inherit God's Kingdom, "They shall see His face, and His name shall be on their foreheads." I John 3:2 reads, "We shall be like Him, for we shall see Him as He is."

Words to Chew On: Prayer opens our eyes to spiritual reality; it's hard for us to hear God and see his power at work when we are full of the lusts of the spirit that Galatians 5:19 talks about. Many are guilty of hearing, but not understanding, and seeing yet not perceiving, for their hearts have grown dull, their ears are hard of hearing, and their eyes they have closed lest they should see with their eyes and hear with their ears, lest they should understand with their hearts and turn, so that God should heal them. Matthew 13:14, 15 Body is the temple of the Lord... I Corinthians 6:19; 3:16. It's not what comes out of the heart defiles man Matthew 15:18-20. "Therefore come out from them and be separate, says the Lord.

Touch no unclean thing, and I will receive you." (2 Corinthian 6:17 NIV)

Prayer: Father, I confess that I've allowed my flesh to take control over me instead of allowing your Holy Spirit to control me. Please, help me to "Draw near to [you] and [you] will draw near to [me]." 2 Corinthians 7:1. Help me to allow your Word to dwell in me so that I can purify myself from everything that contaminates this body and spirit you've given me. Let me open my spiritual eyes and ears Ephesians 3:17-19. I pray that, being rooted and established in love, that I may have power, together with all the Lord's holy people, to grasp how wide and long and high and deep is the love of Christ, and to know this love that surpasses knowledge that you may be filled to the measure of all the fullness of God. 2 Corinthian 6:17

Day 14

CRITICAL SPIRIT

<u>Song</u> : "He Is Lord" HillSong

<u>Scripture Reference:</u> Numbers 12:1-16

Miriam and Aaron spoke against Moses because of the Cushite woman whom he had married, for he had married a Cushite woman. 2 And they said, "Has the Lord indeed spoken only through Moses? Has he not spoken through us also?" And the Lord heard it. 3 Now the man Moses was very meek, more than all people who were on the face of the earth. 4 And suddenly the Lord said to Moses and to Aaron and Miriam, "Come out, you three, to the tent of meeting." And the three of them came out. 5 And the Lord came down in a pillar of cloud and stood at the entrance of the tent and called Aaron and Miriam, and they both came forward. 6 And he said, "Hear my words: If there is a prophet among you, I the Lord make myself known to him in a vision; I speak with him in a dream. 7 Not so with my servant Moses. He is faithful in all my house. 8 With him I speak mouth to mouth, clearly, and not in riddles, and he beholds the form of the Lord. Why then were you not afraid to speak against my servant Moses?" 9 And the anger of the Lord was kindled against them, and he departed.

10 When the cloud removed from over the tent, behold, Miriam was leprous, like snow. And Aaron turned toward Miriam, and behold, she was leprous. 11 And Aaron said to Moses, "Oh, my lord, do not punish us because we have done foolishly and have sinned. 12 Let her not be as one dead, whose flesh is half eaten away when he comes out of his mother's womb." 13 And Moses cried to the Lord, "O God, please heal her—please." 14 But the Lord said to Moses, "If her father had but spit in her face, should she not be shamed seven days? Let her be shut outside the camp seven days, and after that she may be brought in again." 15 So Miriam was shut outside the camp seven days, and the people did not set out on the march till Miriam was brought in again. 16 After that the people set out from Hazeroth and camped in the wilderness of Paran.

Problem in the World: After one too many arguments, I learned that early on in my marriage, my husband felt like I criticized everything he did and everything that he said. I found myself taking my husband on many *why* trips : *"Why did you do that? Why did you do it that way? Why don't you do it this way? Why won't you do this? Why won't you pray with me? Why? Why? Why?"* As I replay my foolish why trips, I wouldn't want to be around me, let alone pray with me either. Later in my marriage, I felt like my husband was critical of everything I said or did that involved our children. The criticism from both of us was the root of some of the turmoil we've experienced in our marriage.

Do you overly criticize others for how they do or say things or maybe in the styles of clothes they wear? Do you judge others for the money they make, political affiliation, or where they live? Do you find yourself always finding fault with something or someone who doesn't meet any of your standards? Is it difficult for you to see the positive in a person or a situation? If you answered yes, to any of these questions then recognize that you have a critical spirit. A critical spirit is a negative attitude of the heart that seeks to condemn, tear down, and destroy with words. A critical spirit creates blind spots in a person's heart and mind causing them to believe they are being constructive. Unfortunately, too many people are critical of their leaders whom they chose as their pastor. They criticize every decision the pastor makes. The Lord is displeased.

<u>Problem in the Text:</u> Miriam and Aaron were talking about their brother, not only their brother but their leader Moses. A conversation had probably sounded a little something like this: Wait, doesn't God speak to us too and not just to Moses? Who does he think he is marrying that Cushite woman? The Lord was not pleased with Miriam's and Aaron's grumbling against, God's servant, Moses. They really thought they knew better than their leader and that the Lord had endowed them with superior wisdom. Miriam's critical spirit caused the Israelites not to march on. On the account of Miriam and Aaron, the Lord removed the cloud and departed from the Israelites.

<u>Solution to the Text</u>: Although the Lord made Miriam leprous and banned her from the camp for seven days as though her father would spit in her face, He allowed her to return to the camp and resume her position. In fact, the Lord still chose to use Miriam for his glory. "The Lord disciplines him whom He loves." Hebrews 12:6

<u>Solution to the World:</u> The Lord calls us sons and daughters. Like our parents in the natural who discipline us when we are out of line, so the Lord disciplines us. We must embrace the fact that if the Lord wanted people to act, think, and behave in the same manner as you and I, He would have made us like robots. I realize that it took a lot of grace and patience

to understand that everyone cooks differently than I do, handles situations differently, and is just not me. We need to give more affirmations to each other and concentrate on the things people do well! How could I expect my husband to build me up when I was tearing him down? Unlike people who remember only the bad and not the good you do, God's love for us remains the same. Hebrews 13:8

Words to Chew On: In contrast, constructive criticism involves opinions that are meant to build up. Be careful how you put your mouth on the man or woman of God, especially if they watch over your soul. Can they give an accurate account to the Lord about you with joy? You don't know who God is preparing to become the next pastor or Bishop, so you should be careful of being critical of any believer. We can't just do and say anything that we want, just because we can. "We were bought with a price, so we are to glorify God in our spirit and body." I Corinthians 6:20.

We must pray for our leaders. We are warned, "Touch not my anointed and do my prophets no harm" I Chronicles 16:22. I realize that I exemplified disrespect to my husband, (my head and covering) by questioning his every move. In addition, when I challenged his manhood in front of my children, that almost was likened to what Miriam and Aaron did in front of the people they were leading who looked up to them. I've since humbly apologized to my husband and children and told my children (especially my daughter) how they should talk to their spouse. We must learn how to stay in our own lane by doing what God has called us to do, without concerning ourselves with how others do what God has called them to do.

<u>Prayer:</u> Holy Spirit, help me to examine my heart. Forgive me for my critical spirit of others. Show me, ME! I tear down every stronghold in my life and, take it captive to the obedience of Christ. Shut the mouths of every negative person who have come against me and my leader. Thank you for giving me a wonderful leader who prays for me and who corrects me when I'm in error and who has my best interest at heart. Teach me how to see others the way you see them. Teach me how to have a heart for your people. Thank you, Lord that despite any criticism that I've allowed to enter my life, you still have a plan and a purpose for me and you still want to use me. Thank you for forgiving me. Amen.

Day 15

BITTERNESS

Song "Amazing Grace" Hymn

Scripture Reference(s): Luke 15:11-32

11 And he said, "There was a man who had two sons. 12 And the younger of them said to his father, 'Father, give me the share of property that is coming to me.' And he divided his property between them. 13 Not many days later, the younger son gathered all he had and took a journey into a far country, and there he squandered his property in reckless living. 14 And when he had spent everything, a severe famine arose in that country, and he began to be in need. 15 So he went and hired himself out to one of the citizens of that country, who sent him into his fields to feed pigs. 16 And he was longing to be fed with the pods that the pigs ate, and no one gave him anything. 17 "But when he came to himself, he said, 'How many of my father's hired servants have more than enough

bread, but I perish here with hunger! 18 I will arise and go to my father, and I will say to him, "Father, I have sinned against heaven and before you. 19 I am no longer worthy to be called your son. Treat me as one of your hired servants."' 20 And he arose and came to his father. But while he was still a long way off, his father saw him and felt compassion, and ran and embraced him and kissed him. 21 And the son said to him, 'Father, I have sinned against heaven and before you. I am no longer worthy to be called your son.' 22 But the father said to his servants, 'Bring quickly the best robe, and put it on him, and put a ring on his hand, and shoes on his feet. 23 And bring the fattened calf and kill it, and let us eat and celebrate. 24 For this my son was dead, and is alive again; he was lost, and is found.' And they began to celebrate. 25 "Now his older son was in the field, and as he came and drew near to the house, he heard music and dancing. 26 And he called one of the servants and asked what these things meant. 27 And he said to him, 'Your brother has come, and your father has killed the fattened calf, because he has received him back safe and sound.' 28 But he was angry and refused to go in. His father came out and entreated him, 29 but he answered his father, 'Look, these many years I have served you, and I never disobeyed your command, yet you never gave me a young goat, that I might celebrate with my friends. 30 But when this son of yours came, who has devoured your property

with prostitutes, you killed the fattened calf for him!'
31 And he said to him, 'Son, you are always with me,
and all that is mine is yours. 32 It was fitting to celebrate and be glad, for this your brother was dead,
and is alive; he was lost, and is found.'"

Problem in the World: Many people are sick or experiencing a spiritual death because they have a root
of bitterness in their heart which is likened to poison.
Poison is a substance capable of causing the illness or
death of a living thing when it is ingested or absorbed
in the body. An illustration of this would be likened to
a plant which has roots that supplies food and water
to the rest of the plant for growth. On the contrary, a
poisonous plant when ingested or touched will choke
the life out of a living thing causing death or illness.
When the roots of a plant are uprooted, the plant will
no longer grow. Most people who have been raped
or abused have reported some type of bitterness. It's
not the rape or abuse itself, but the bitterness and
unhealthy feelings that build up within a person who
has been violated. It has often been said that "hurt
people, hurt people." A person may not express hurt
on the outside, but rather hold onto the hurtful feelings inside of their inner man where it festers and
grows into bitterness. Demonic spirits gain access
into a person's life who have been hurt and plant evil
seeds that sprout into roots of bitterness. The root
of bitterness moves through a person's being and

develop many spiritual, mental and even physical bondages that stump a person's growth.

Problem in the Text: The young son was ready to flex his wings, get out of the house, go buck wild and party. He wanted his inheritance early which meant that he would only get a third of his portion. In the Jewish culture, it was like saying he'd wished his father was dead. He went to live on his own, but in due time his money ran out. He had to take a job feeding the pigs which was a form of humiliation in the Jewish culture. The younger son squandered all the money he had by spending it all. The oldest son carried a "chip on his shoulder" or bitterness. He felt that he was the one who remained working by his father's side for years, and then his younger brother comes back and got the royal treatment.

Solution to the Text: The younger son came to his senses and realized that even his father's servants live and eat better than what he was doing., so he decided to return to his father as a hired hand. The father welcomed his younger son before he even arrived, his father demanded a feast and had his servants clothe his son with best clothes.

Solution to the World: God is rich in mercy Psalm 145:8; Ephesians 2:4-10 But God, being rich in mercy, because of the great love with which he loved us, [5] even when we were dead in our trespasses, made us alive together with Christ—by grace you have been saved— [6] and raised us up with him and seated us with him in the heavenly places in Christ Jesus,[7] so that in the coming ages he might show the immeasurable riches of his grace in kindness toward us in Christ Jesus. [8] For by grace you have been saved through faith. And this is not your own doing; it is the gift of God, [9] not a result of works, so that no one may boast. [10] For we are his workmanship, created in Christ Jesus for good works, which God prepared beforehand, that we should walk in them.

Words to Chew On: See to it that no one fails to obtain the grace of God; that no "root of bitterness" springs up and causes trouble, and by it many become defiled.

Prayer: Father, I confess that I have bitterness in my heart because_____. Help me to see that person as you see them. I need you, to root out bitterness and restore the joy of my salvation. Make me whole. In Jesus' name, amen.

Day 16

IDOL WORSHIP

<u>Song:</u> "Honor and Glory" (To the king eternal immortal invisible the only God) Billy Funk- Hosanna! Music

<u>Scripture Reference:</u> Acts 17:22-31

22 So Paul, standing in the midst of the Areopagus, said: "Men of Athens, I perceive that in every way you are very religious. 23 For as I passed along and observed the objects of your worship, I found also an altar with this inscription: 'To the unknown god.' What therefore you worship as unknown, this I proclaim to you. 24 The God who made the world and everything in it, being Lord of heaven and earth, does not live in temples made by man, 25 nor is he served by human hands, as though he needed anything, since he himself gives to all mankind life and breath and everything. 26 And he made from one man every nation of mankind to live on all the face of the earth, having determined allotted periods and the boundaries of

their dwelling place, 27 that they should seek God, and perhaps feel their way toward him and find him. Yet he is actually not far from each one of us, 28 for "'In him we live and move and have our being'; as even some of your own poets have said, For we are indeed his offspring.'

29 Being then God's offspring, we ought not to think that the divine being is like gold or silver or stone, an image formed by the art and imagination of man. 30 The times of ignorance God overlooked, but now he commands all people everywhere to repent, 31 because he has fixed a day on which he will judge the world in righteousness by a man whom he has appointed; and of this he has given assurance to all by raising him from the dead."

Problem in the World: The body of Christ is guilty of idolizing men and women of God and which keeps us from experiencing true worship. An idol is anything or anyone whom we reference more than God. There are people or fans or will travel all over the country to follow preachers, music artists, and notable speakers. I'm not saying that there is anything the matter with following those who may add value to your life. However, it becomes a problem when people faint at the feet of mere mortal men; bow before them and reach out to touch them like they are gold. It's amazing how many Christians reverence man, or their jobs, hobbies, education, and more over God. People are looking to be entertained with music in church, looking for celebrity choirs, yet many Christians are not having a pure worship.

Problem in the Text: Paul walked around in Athens while waiting for his Christian brothers. He saw statues and stones which made references to other gods. He was disturbed when he saw the unknown god inscription. The Greeks believed in many gods, for they were a polytheistic society and Paul was disturbed when he saw the stone that said to the unknown god.

Solution to the World: Thank God that there is no temptation that is not common to man...but he provides a way of escape...I Cor.10:13

Solution to the Text: Paul reasoned with philosophers who he said was also religious that the unknown God is the creator, divine creator not built by hands nothing by what man can do. Had it not been for Christ coming to take the sins of the world we wouldn't have our being. A few years after the crucifixion of Christ and after Paul's conversion to Christianity, Paul was able to boldly proclaim: "It's in Him that we live move and have our being." Behold the Lamb of the world who comes to take away the sins of the world.

<u>Words to Chew On:</u> Christians must know the one and only true God. There will come a time where God will separate the wheat from the tare. In the movie <u>God is Not Dead</u>, it's about a story where a young man in a university stood up to the professor's challenge to prove that God is Not Dead. The professor of philosophy made everyone in class sign that God is Dead in order to get a passing grade. The young man set out to prove that God is alive and well when he refused to sign like all others. Also, I am reminded of a story during evangelism outreach. While passing out tracts, a young lady dressed in Muslim garb was waiting for the bus with her son and a little baby in the stroller. She appeared to be occupied with her phone and refused a tract when asked by motioning her hands no. Meanwhile, the little boy who looked like six years old asked for a tract. He pleaded, "I want one, can I have one." Mom motioned okay through nonverbal communication that we had permission to meet the boy's request as we made eye contact for approval. We proceeded up the street and returned. The little boy noticed the colorful bracelet that I was wearing and asked what it was. Again, we (my outreach partner and I) sought permission from mom to proceed and mom consented with a nod, all the while still on the phone. We shared the gospel with the little boy and he wanted to invite Jesus into his heart. Mom allowed us to pray with her son. Apparently, Mom was idolizing whoever was on the phone. Her

attention was so diverted to the other end of the call that right after the son invited Christ into his life, their bus came. I couldn't help but rejoice and think, "Does this woman know what she just did?"

Prayer: Forgive me for not reverencing you as the one and only true God. Your Word says that." you are a jealous God. Please forgive me for putting _____ before you which has kept me from spending time in your Word and in your presence in worship. Lord, you said I shall not have no other gods before you and I confess that I have made_____ my idol. Exodus 20:3-5. Lord, let me give only you my undivided attention. I want to spend time with you daily at this time_____. Thank you for removing this heart of bitterness.

Day 17

SPIRITUAL DISTRACTION

<u>Song</u> "Be Still and Know that I am God" Hymn

<u>Scripture Reference:</u> Luke 10:38-42

38 Now as they went on their way, Jesus entered a village. And a woman named Martha welcomed him into her house. 39 And she had a sister called Mary, who sat at the Lord's feet and listened to his teaching. 40 But Martha was distracted with much serving. And she went up to him and said, "Lord, do you not care that my sister has left me to serve alone? Tell her then to help me." 41 But the Lord answered her, "Martha, Martha, you are anxious and troubled about many things, 42 but one thing is necessary. Mary has chosen the good portion, which will not be taken away from her."

<u>Problem in the World</u>: A lot of Christians are like the tuning into of AM radio stations, where the frequency usually does not allow for good reception. We have so many distractions that make it difficult to hear the voice of God: business meetings, taking/attending

to our children's activities, work, sports, entertainment and social media. I was in a church service in which I saw adults and children using their phone to play apps while worship music was playing. Many Christians spend time week in and week out and still have no sign of a change of heart. There are some-timey Christians (go to church sometimes) who are honorary CEM members; they only go to church on Christmas, Easter, and Mother's Day. CEM members enjoy hearing the word preached, yet still live as the world does because the devil has a foothold over them. Many will say, "I'm about to pray," but then find a thousand and one reasons to do something else. Matters that should be handled in the spirit, many try to handle in the flesh. I saw a post by a professing Christian indicating that he would "beat the devil's a—" the post further stated that he was going through tough times and God was testing him, yet he negate to continue fellowship with the saints. Many Christians mistake busyness for productivity, another tactic of the enemy.

Problem in the Text: Martha sought to do things according to tradition of entertaining guests from the world's perspective. She looked at her sister Mary, who appeared to not be working, in comparison to what she was doing. Martha thought Mary should have been helping her cook and clean.

<u>Solution to the Text:</u> Jesus rebuked Martha and basically told Martha to leave Mary alone because she sought the greater things which was to humbly be in the presence of the Lord and to be taught of Him.

<u>Solution to the World</u>: The Word tells us to, "Be still and know that I am God. I will be exalted among the nations, I will be exalted in the earth!" Psalm 46:10 Christ came to the earth for us to have a relationship with Him. Christ gave us the greatest gift and the greatest gift we can give back to Christ is our lives.

<u>Words to Chew On:</u> The enemy has deceived us into putting off our relationship of prayer and worship time with the Lord by allowing us to think we should be texting during service or watching social media sites as soon as we wake up in the morning. Our fight is not against flesh and blood but spiritual wickedness in high places. Ephesians 6:12. While working on this devotional, I was pulled in many directions. Many were assignments that I'd taken on and not assignments God gave me, which delayed the process. Some distractions we cause upon ourselves others are from the enemy. Toward the final edit of this devotional, my goal was to spend a great deal of time typing. However, I sprained my dominant arm and a couple of days later I fell off a bike and injured my wrist on the other side of my arm. I recognize that was a tactic of the enemy because I was in writhing

pain and could barely type. More time was spent going to the doctor to have x-rays, elevating and icing my arms. God is trying to speak to us, but we can't hear him while we are busy fulfilling other people's dreams and we have become unproductive. What are the things that are distracting you from spending quality time with the Lord? If you are continuously on the move remember that we are too busy not to pray and seek the Word for our lives.

Prayer: Father, forgive me for being distracted and making other things a priority that really aren't helping me to fulfill the assignments you've called me to. Help me to know that entrepreneurship is about serving others and it's a calling from you. I bind up the spirit of distraction in my marriage, with my children, in my finances, and doing what others want me to do. Help me to focus on what really matters and that's you. Thank you, for hearing my prayer. In Jesus' Name, Amen.

Day 18

THE WORD

Song: "Your Words" Third Day

Scripture Reference: Luke 8:4-15

4 And when a great crowd was gathering and people from town after town came to him, he said in a parable, 5 "A sower went out to sow his seed. And as he sowed, some fell along the path and was trampled underfoot, and the birds of the air devoured it. 6 And some fell on the rock, and as it grew up, it withered away, because it had no moisture. 7 And some fell among thorns, and the thorns grew up with it and choked it. 8 And some fell into good soil and grew and yielded a hundredfold." As he said these things, he called out, "He who has ears to hear, let him hear." 9 And when his disciples asked him what this parable meant, 10 he said, "To you it has been given to know the secrets of the kingdom of God, but for others they are in parables, so that 'seeing they may not see,

and hearing they may not understand.' 11 Now the parable is this: The seed is the word of God. 12 The ones along the path are those who have heard; then the devil comes and takes away the word from their hearts, so that they may not believe and be saved. 13 And the ones on the rock are those who, when they hear the word, receive it with joy. But these have no root; they believe for a while, and in time of testing fall away. 14 And as for what fell among the thorns, they are those who hear, but as they go on their way they are choked by the cares and riches and plea-sures of life, and their fruit does not mature. 15 As for that in the good soil, they are those who, hearing the word, hold it fast in an honest and good heart, and bear fruit with patience.

Problem in the World: Many Christians have for-gotten their testimony or neglect to share when they've accepted the Lord Jesus into their life and there was a noticeable change in them. Reflect on your conversion. What happened that you knew you were changed? Why is it that many Christians have entered a backslidden state? They've adapted a mindset of the world that it's okay to live with someone even if you are not married, it's okay to put yourself in compromising positions that have others question their faith. Many Christians have become hearers of the Word only and not doers. James 1:22. Sadly, a lot of professing Christians only identify in name only. Perhaps, they've never had the proper training. What about Christians who know the Word and still blatantly fulfill the desires of the flesh?

Problem in the Text: The farmer sowed seeds, which represent the Word of God. The seeds (Word of God) fell among various places. Some seeds fell among the path and they were trampled on. Seeds that fell on hard ground indicate the destruction of the enemy to cause hardness of heart toward sin.

The birds came and ate them which represent the devil how he keeps people from believing and being saved. Others fell on the rock.
    The seeds that fell on the rocks were scorched by the sun. They didn't have any moisture so the people who had the word didn't have any depth or deepness to it. Some seeds grew among thorns and as they grew the seeds were choked. The seeds (Word of God) that fell among the thorns represent when the Word goes forth and people become choked by the worries and cares of the world.

Solution to the Text: The last seeds that the farmer threw fell and grew on good soil. The soil seeds that fell on good ground and it produced a fruit thirty and one hundred times. Christ came to earth so that we may have life and have it more abundantly. His Word was in the beginning and the Word was with

God. Hebrews 4:12 tells us that the Word of God is sharper than any two-edged sword and how it corrects, rebukes, and teaches.

Solution to the World: "Be still and know that I am God. I will be exalted among the nations, I will be exalted in the earth!" Psalm 46:10 If anyone hears my words and does not keep them, I do not judge him; for I did not come to judge the world but to save the world. John 12:47. Christ came to the earth for us to have a relationship with Him. Christ gave us the greatest gift and the greatest gift we can give back to Christ is our lives.

Words to Chew On: Don't take Christ for granted. He has given us chance to get it right. Our eyes witnessed the miracle of a boy who was in a wheel chair, walk. We watched God strengthen his legs, walk and praise God on the tambourine.

Prayer: Father, teach me how to rely on Your Word, for "your Word is a lamp unto my feet and a light unto my path." (Ps 119:105). Help me to hide your Word in my heart that I may not sin against you… (Ps 119:11) Open my eyes to hear the truth of your Word. I need you to help me to study Your Word, and rightly divide your truth. (IITim. 2:15) Thank you, for hearing my prayer. In Jesus' Name, Amen.

Day 19

SERVANTHOOD

<u>Song:</u> "I Will Serve Thee" Hymn

<u>Scripture Reference:</u> John 13:1-17

13 Now before the Feast of the Passover, when Jesus knew that his hour had come to depart out of this world to the Father, having loved his own who were in the world, he loved them to the end. 2 During supper, when the devil had already put it into the heart of Judas Iscariot, Simon's son, to betray him, 3 Jesus, knowing that the Father had given all things into his hands, and that he had come from God and was going back to God, 4 rose from supper. He laid aside his outer garments, and taking a towel, tied it around his waist. 5 Then he poured water into a basin and began to wash the disciples' feet and to wipe them with the towel that was wrapped around him. 6 He came to Simon Peter, who said to him, "Lord, do you wash my feet?" 7 Jesus answered him,

"What I am doing you do not understand now, but afterward you will understand." 8 Peter said to him, "You shall never wash my feet." Jesus answered him, "If I do not wash you, you have no share with me." 9 Simon Peter said to him, "Lord, not my feet only but also my hands and my head!" 10 Jesus said to him, "The one who has bathed does not need to wash, except for his feet, but is completely clean. And you are clean, but not every one of you." 11 For he knew who was to betray him; that was why he said, "Not all of you are clean."

12 When he had washed their feet and put on his outer garments and resumed his place, he said to them, "Do you understand what I have done to you? 13 You call me Teacher and Lord, and you are right, for so I am. 14 If I then, your Lord and Teacher, have washed your feet, you also ought to wash one another's feet. 15 For I have given you an example, that you also should do just as I have done to you. 16 Truly, truly, I say to you, a servant is not greater than his master, nor is a messenger greater than the one who sent him. 17 If you know these things, blessed are you if you do them.

Problem in the World: As believers do we have a heart that truly seeks to serve others? Many people have not been taught the value of serving and working for others. Strangely, there is a belief of entitlement, everyone (the world) owes you something. Worship services continue to happen week in and week out. People feel good with the music and preached Word, go home, and go about their business the rest of the week. During the week, are you calling and checking on someone who may have lost a loved one, or sending a thinking of you card to someone, are you seeking ways to help someone in their situation? While waiting in line for pretzels, customers watched a shift in workers take place at the register. The new worker appeared to have an attitude because of a personal interaction. When it was the next person's turn in line, the disgruntled worker failed to greet the customer and only took order in an unpleasant tone. A woman who had been waiting in line for ten minutes with me, politely told me that I could go before her. That gesture made a huge difference in getting back to a running car with a sick child in it.

When was the last time you served someone else and not waiting for others to serve you?

Problem in the Text: Typically, servants washed the feet of those who entered a house.

Solution in the Text: Jesus was about to die on the cross for us, he was about to be betrayed. He takes a towel and wraps it around his waist and begins to wash the disciples' feet, a job that is typically done by servants.

<u>Solution to the World:</u> "The Son of man did not come to serve but to serve and give his life as a ransom for all." Matthew 20:28.

<u>Words to Chew On:</u> Above all else, we are called to serve and not to be served! Jesus even said that himself. Matthew 20:28. Born again Christians, who profess Christ, if the goal of getting into business or a ministry for what appears to be glitz and glamour one is in it for the wrong reason. What a revelation that entrepreneurship is a calling! We are called to serve first and then all these things (finances) shall be added unto us. The harvest is plentiful, but the laborers are few. Matt.9:37 Jesus was the perfect example to serve. Matthew 9:35-38 The story in the Bible talks about when we do anything to the least of these we do it unto God. Matthew 25:31-46

<u>Prayer:</u> Father, forgive me for thinking only of myself. Help me to look to the needs of others as I would myself. Teach me how to love and serve others as if serving you. Father, show me where I can join you at work to meet the needs of others. Amen

Day 20

RACISM

Song "No Greater Love" GMWA Mass Choir

Scripture Reference: Galatians 3:28; John 4:7-15

28 There is neither Jew nor Greek, there is neither slave nor free, there is no male and female, for you are all one in Christ Jesus.

7 A woman from Samaria came to draw water. Jesus said to her, "Give me a drink." 8 (For his disciples had gone away into the city to buy food.) 9 The Samaritan woman said to him, "How is it that you, a Jew, ask for a drink from me, a woman of Samaria?" (For Jews have no dealings with Samaritans.) 10 Jesus answered her, "If you knew the gift of God, and who it is that is saying to you, 'Give me a drink,' you would have asked him, and he would have given you living water." 11 The woman said to him, "Sir, you have nothing to draw water with, and the well is deep. Where do you get that living water? 12 Are

you greater than our father Jacob? He gave us the well and drank from it himself, as did his sons and his livestock." 13 Jesus said to her, "Everyone who drinks of this water will be thirsty again, 14 but who- ever drinks of the water that I will give him will never be thirsty again. The water that I will give him will become in him a spring of water welling up to eternal life." 15 The woman said to him, "Sir, give me this water, so that I will not be thirsty or have to come here to draw water."

Problem in the World: Racism is an evil that plagues our society. After many years of segregation in America, the body of Christ is still separated! Not only are many churches separated by ethnicity, but many (Holy Ghost filled, fire baptized, tongue speaking) Christians have participated in the involve- ment of dehumanizing their brothers and sisters in Christ when they speak ill of the other with deroga- tory comments whether unintentional or intentional. Most people who are ignorant to the device of the enemy assume that all Asian food is "Chinese food," or all Latinos are from "Puerto Rican land" or all dark and brown skinned people are "black" and are iden- tified as African Americans. Rev. Dr. Martin Luther King, Jr., one of the greatest civil rights leader gave the infamous, "I Have A Dream Speech." He believed in equality for all of mankind. Many people claim that they are not a racist, but in many cases it is hidden and comes through in a subtle manner.

Problem in the Text: Both scripture references elude to a culture divide even in biblical times.

Solution to the Text: Jesus showed great concern for the Samaritan woman, a group of people whom Jews did not associate with.

Solution to the World: Jesus' love is for all, not just one group of people.

Words to Chew On: Christ broke through all racial and cultural barriers. Who are we to put our nationality above all others? "It is He who has made us and not we ourselves." Psalm 100:3 We must be mindful how we think and of what we speak of all people. Are you guilty of making jokes about people from another race? Which of your words edified or did it tear down? As a missionary during my college years, I've had the distinct pleasure to stay in the homes and churches of Christians who were Filipino, Native American, Anglo Saxon, and Japanese. What an enriching experience!

Prayer: Father, open my eyes to see the racial prejudices that I have in my heart. Please forgive me for thinking of myself and my race as superior than another. I denounce every evil that promote hatred and disdain toward any of my fellow laborers in Christ. Thank you, Lord, for washing me clean from any form of racism. In Jesus' Name. Amen.

Day 21

PURPOSE

Song: "I Know the Plans I Have For You"
Martha Munizzi

Scripture Reference(s): Jeremiah 29:11;
Matthew 16:13-16

11 For I know the plans I have for you, declares the Lord, plans for welfare[a] and not for evil, to give you a future and a hope.

Peter Confesses Jesus as the Christ

13 Now when Jesus came into the district of Caesarea Philippi, he asked his disciples, "Who do people say that the Son of Man is?" 14 And they said, "Some say John the Baptist, others say Elijah, and others Jeremiah or one of the prophets." 15 He said to them, "But who do you say that I am?" 16 Simon Peter replied, "You are the Christ, the Son of the living God."

<u>Problem in the World:</u> I am reminded of the popular movie, The Matrix, a computer-generated dream world that was designed to keep humans under control. Much like our government system, our prison system, and the prison of our minds. In the movie, the character Neo, played by actor Keanu Reeves was a computer programmer by day known as Thomas Anderson and a hacker by night as Neo. He was feeling empty like there had to be more to life. He didn't know his worth and purpose. He didn't know that he was destined for greatness. Like Neo, so many don't know that they are destined for greatness because they've listened to lies from the enemy who has told them time and time again, "You are nothing," "You don't measure up like ____,",or "You can't do or have that because..." Many accept life as it is, doing the mundane things such as going to work day in and day out, going to church week after week feeling unfulfilled and having no change. Neo was offered a choice to accept his life as it was by taking the blue pill, or he could find out if there really was more to life by accepting the red pill. Too often we take what life throws our way and don't realize that we have a choice to stay stuck or move ahead. Many of us are imprisoned in our thinking like Neo. "See you messed up, again, God doesn't want you, who is going to want you." Anything that is not in the Word of God is a lie. We are held in bondage. How does one act when not free. These problems keep

us from experiencing the freedom God intended us to walk in. The character Neo chose the red pill which allowed him to enter the Matrix. Once inside, he discovered that he was the "Chosen One," the savior, the one to save the people and lead them to freedom. He had the potential to stop the cycle of mass extinction of humans. "Choice not chance determines your destiny." Like Neo, many of us are not aware of the greatness that lie in us. Many of us have people assigned to us that we need to help move them to their destiny but they can't get to their destiny because we are not in position where God has called us. Neo didn't know his worth and had yet to discover his purpose. Once Neo chose to believe and accept the words repeated to him by Morpheus (played by Laurence Fishbourne) and Trinity (played by Carrie-Ann Moss), he accepted his role and rose to assume even greater powers.

Problem in the Text: The Israelites were taken captive into a foreign land. Their identity had been stolen and they had to assimilate into another culture. Many speculated who they thought Jesus the Christ was.

Solution to the Text: In the midst of living in a foreign land, the Lord told the Israelites to build houses and to marry because He [still] had a plan for them in spite of what the situation appeared to be. Christ wanted to ensure that the disciples knew who He was and not listen to hearsay. Flesh and blood could not have revealed that Jesus is the Christ.

Solution to the World: Christ came to fulfill his purpose. The Bible is evident of people full of purpose and they didn't even know it. Take for example, Moses, who was raised as an Egyptian with a stuttering condition; yet, Moses was the one whom the Lord appointed to lead the people out of Egypt (Exodus 3); look at Gideon, the least of the tribe of Benjamin, in whom the Lord used to lead 300 men versus the 32,000 men he thought he needed to defeat the Midianites (Judges 7); then, Saul went out to look for his father's donkey and becoming a king was the furthest thing from his mind when the prophet anointed him (I Samuel 9).

Words to Chew On: Who do you say that you are? What are some areas that you are you are really good at? I'm here to tell you that there is more to life and that you are a valuable gift to the body of Christ. Here to remind you that Jeremiah 29:11 says that God has a plan for you. People can't go to their destiny because we are not walking in our purpose. People are assigned to us. Jesus's purpose was to seek that which was lost. His assignment was you and me when He hung on the tree. When Jesus took the sins of the world upon himself, he became cursed. We must remind ourselves who we are and whose we are according to the Word of God. "You are a royal priesthood, a chosen generation." I Peter 2:9

Prayer: Father, help me to realize my purpose and to fulfill it. Father, you know my destiny, help me to walk in what you have called me to do and be. I need the guidance of the Holy Spirit to direct my path. Lord, I need you and I can't do anything without you. Show me the resources and people whom I need to connect with. I recognize that apart from you I am nothing. I declare and decree that I am the head and not the tail, above and not beneath. Deuteronomy 28:13. Thank you, Lord for showing me my future. Use my gifts and talents for your glory. In Jesus' Name Amen.

Day 22

FAITH

<u>Song</u> "Great is thy Faithfulness" Hymn

<u>Scripture Reference:</u> Matthew 17:14-20; Hebrews 11:1

14 And when they came to the crowd, a man came up to him and, kneeling before him, 15 said, "Lord, have mercy on my son, for he has seizures and he suffers terribly. For often he falls into the fire, and often into the water. 16 And I brought him to your disciples, and they could not heal him." 17 And Jesus answered, "O faithless and twisted generation, how long am I to be with you? How long am I to bear with you? Bring him here to me." 18 And Jesus rebuked the demon, and it came out of him, and the boy was healed instantly. 19 Then the disciples came to Jesus privately and said, "Why could we not cast it out?" 20 He said to them, "Because of your little faith. For truly, I say to you, if you have faith like a grain of mustard seed, you will

say to this mountain, 'Move from here to there,' and it will move, and nothing will be impossible for you."

"Now faith is the assurance of things hoped for, the conviction of things not seen." Hebrews 11:1

Problem in the World: There is a story about a Mountain Climber who wanted recognition for climbing the Aconcagua on his own. After years of preparation, he set out for his journey in which he had not anticipated camping out. He loosened the ropes to climb down, but he began to swing and plummet. While plummeting in the air, he felt himself jolted and caught onto something that had him hanging on and swinging by the rope. The mountain climber cried out to God to save him. A deep voice from heaven asked if the climber really wanted to be saved and the climber answered, "Yes." The voice then told the climber to, "Let go of the rope," but the climber grew still and didn't respond. The very next day, the climber was found frozen to death, two feet from the ground. So many Christians lack true faith. They fear not having enough food, money, clothes, talent or the ability to do certain jobs because of what everything around them looks like.

Problem in the Text: After the disciples watched Jesus perform many miracles and they walked with him, they lacked faith still. Jesus used the disciples' weakness to cast out the demon to show that we must completely rely on Christ's strength and not our own.

<u>Solution to the Text:</u> Jesus rebuked the demon and it came out. Jesus always fasted and prayed. He told the disciples that they were unable to cast it out because prayer and fasting were needed for that kind to go out.

<u>Solution to the World:</u> Christ can heal all manner of sickness and disease, but do you have the faith to believe? On many accounts before Jesus healed people, He told them that their faith had made them well. Jesus asked the lame man who came to the pool for 38 years, "Do you want to be made whole?" The lesson we can draw from this story is that, once people make a conscious decision that they want to be healed, it is then Jesus will heal them. Jesus told the man who was paralyzed "Your faith has made you whole." John 5:6. No matter what situation we face, it must line up with the Word of the Lord because at the name of Jesus every knee must bow and confess that He is Lord! Philippians 2:10. "I can do the things that Jesus did and have the things his Word says we can have. Christ tells believers that. If we have faith as a mustard seed, we can say to any mountain to be removed and it shall be moved from here to there. Romans 14:11.

Words to Chew On: We have the resurrection power living inside of us, which means we can speak to our situation! Because of the power and blood of Jesus Christ, Jesus said greater works shall we do. Without faith it is impossible to please God. Hebrews 11:6-8. We must exercise our faith, which is a spiritual muscle. Faith is critical to the Christian believer. When we vacillate between faith and doubt, the Bible says that we are unstable in all of our ways. Faith is the substance hoped for and the evidence not seen. Hebrews 11:1.

Prayer: Father, help me to have faith in You, for Your Word, and in Your power. You continue to prove yourself to me through trials you have brought me through, I know it no one else but You. Oh, Lord, my Strength and Redeemer; build me up where I am weak! Thank you, Lord Jesus, for a new level of faith in You. I declare and decree that I will live and not die and declare the work of the Lord. Psalm 118:17. In Jesus's Name Amen.

Day 23

HOPE

<u>Song:</u> "The Solid Rock" Hymn

<u>Scripture Reference:</u> I Kings 17:8 -14

8 Then the word of the Lord came to him, 9 "Arise, go to Zarephath, which belongs to Sidon, and dwell there. Behold, I have commanded a widow there to feed you." 10 So he arose and went to Zarephath. And when he came to the gate of the city, behold, a widow was there gathering sticks. And he called to her and said, "Bring me a little water in a vessel, that I may drink." 11 And as she was going to bring it, he called to her and said, "Bring me a morsel of bread in your hand." 12 And she said, "As the Lord your God lives, I have nothing baked, only a handful of flour in a jar and a little oil in a jug. And now I am gathering a couple of sticks that I may go in and prepare it for myself and my son, that we may eat it and die." 13 And Elijah said to her, "Do not fear; go and do as

you have said. But first make me a little cake of it and bring it to me, and afterward make something for yourself and your son. 14 For thus says the Lord, the God of Israel, 'The jar of flour shall not be spent, and the jug of oil shall not be empty, until the day that the Lord sends rain upon the earth.'.

Problem in the World: Many people feel hopeless, helpless, powerless, oppressed, and in despair. Perhaps, the loss of a job or the burnout of having one, the loss of a loved one, living conditions, finances, and relationships have one to feel like there is no way out and that there is no hope for their situation. One day while driving to work, I listened to a caller on the radio share her testimony about how she overcame drug addiction. She mentioned that when she used drugs and attempted suicide, it wasn't to hurt anyone but to emasculate the pain that she had endured in her life.

Problem in the Text: The widow was prepared to die with her son after they baked their last meal, so she thought.

Solution in the Text: The widow and her household was able to live off the cakes for several days.. It seemed like all hope was gone when the widow told the prophet she was about to scrounge up enough food to eat her last meal. It seemed like all hope was gone when the woman lost her son.

Solution to the World: I have come that you may have life and have it more abundantly. Christ came so that our suffering would not be eternal; salvation is not based on whether we are happy or sad or grieving or not grieving…John 16:33 Jesus tells us to take heart because He has overcome the world. I have said these things to you, that in me you may have peace. In the world you will have tribulation. But take heart; I have overcome the world."

Words to Chew On: We are more than conquerors in all these things and "there is a light at the end of the tunnel."

Prayer: Father, thank you that you are the same yesterday today and forever. Thank you that you are the resurrection and the life. I'm asking you to give me hope in the midst of the storm. Thank you that nothing shall separate me from the love of Christ. Romans 8:35-39

Day 24

PEACE

Song: "Tomorrow" Winans

Scripture Reference(s): Luke 2:8-20 John 14:27

8 And in the same region there were shepherds out in the field, keeping watch over their flock by night. 9 And an angel of the Lord appeared to them, and the glory of the Lord shone around them, and they were filled with great fear. 10 And the angel said to them, "Fear not, for behold, I bring you good news of great joy that will be for all the people. 11 For unto you is born this day in the city of David a Savior, who is Christ the Lord. 12 And this will be a sign for you: you will find a baby wrapped in swaddling cloths and lying in a manger." 13 And suddenly there was with the angel a multitude of the heavenly host praising God and saying,

14 "Glory to God in the highest,
    and on earth peace among those with whom
    he is pleased!"

15 When the angels went away from them into heaven, the shepherds said to one another, "Let us go over to Bethlehem and see this thing that has happened, which the Lord has made known to us." 16 And they went with haste and found Mary and Joseph, and the baby lying in a manger. 17 And when they saw it, they made known the saying that had been told them concerning this child. 18 And all who heard it wondered at what the shepherds told them. 19 But Mary treasured up all these things, pondering them in her heart. 20 And the shepherds returned, glorifying and praising God for all they had heard and seen, as it had been told them.

Problem in the World: Do you have peace? We are given a nice nativity scene how Jesus entered the world. Many were looking for the Christ child to come in a palace and with fancy clothes and jewelry. Many people are unsettled about life issues: marriage, children, jobs, relationships, churches, and family. The tragic story of actor Robin Williams' death is an example of one appearing to have it all, but battling internal conflict of unrest.

Problem in the Text: Mary went into labor when she and Joseph were turned away from the inn. Jesus' birth really was not good news to many. It was to the point that when the emperor found out that Jesus would be born he ordered all Jewish male children from birth to about two years old to be killed.

Solution to the Text: Jesus came in a dirty cave which was used as an animal feeding. The place was dark and dirty; everyone was looking for Jesus to come through a palace. He came through humble beginnings. Jesus was born, died and resurrected. The chastisement of our peace was upon Him.

Solution to the World: Christ grew up ascended into heaven died was buried and resurrected. Christ gives us peace that surpasses all understanding. My peace I give you not as the world gives

Words to Chew On: There is a slogan which says, No Jesus No Peace, Know Jesus Know Peace. He is coming back He opened the way for peace with God and paid the price for sin Christ coming back and will rule the world. Do you long for peace? Is Christ Lord of your life?

Prayer: Father, thank you that you are able to give me peace. Help me to cast all my cares upon you because you care for me. I Peter 5:7 Amen.

Day 25

LOVE

Song: "For God So Loved the World" Vanessa Bell Armstrong

Scripture Reference(s): John 3:16; I John 4:7,8

Problem in the World: Many people are looking for love and seeking it in all the wrong places: drugs, alcohol, sex, people, and more; they will go to extremes for love. Many woman think that having a baby they will be loved, some go after men who will take care of them, yet they may be treated dishonorably. There was a study that observed behaviors of a baby monkey who did not receive any human touch versus the baby monkey who received care.

Problem in the Text: God did not come to seek the good but that which was lost; did not come to condemn the world but through him the world may be saved; a man had to lose his life, Greater love has no one than to lay down his life for a friend

Solution to the Text: Christ (love) is; I John 4:7, 8 Beloved let us love one another for love is of God. He who loveth not, knows not God for God is love.

Solution to the World: ↑There is nothing that we can do to earn Christ's love. He is a jealous God. His love is deeper than the ocean for us. While we were yet sinners, Christ died for us.

Words to Chew On: In spite of our inadequacies, failures, and sins, Jesus Christ paid for our sins. The chastisement of our peace was upon His shoulders. The Father loves you through it all and still has a plan and purpose for you. Romans 8:38 tells us that nothing can separate us from the love of God.

Prayer: Father, help me to know your unconditional love that you have for me. Thank you for your love, the greatest gift. Amen

Day 26

FEAR

<u>Song:</u> "God Has Not Given Us the Spirit of Fear" Stephen Hurd/"Trust In You" Anthony Brown and Group Therapy

<u>Scripture Reference(s):</u> II Timothy 1:7 Joshua 1:10-11 Moses the servant died, but God tells Joshua to carry on and take this people, to the land which I am giving to them—the children of Israel Be strong and of courage and know that I will never leave you nor will I forsake you. II Timothy 1:7

And Joshua commanded the officers of the people, 11 "Pass through the midst of the camp and command the people, 'Prepare your provisions, for within three days you are to pass over this Jordan to go in to take possession of the land that the Lord your God is giving you to possess.'"

<u>Problem in the World</u>: What is holding you back from the things God called you to do? Do you aspire to sing, aspire to act, aspire to dance, aspire to write, aspire to go back to school? Many of us have many aspirations we are watching other people have success. It was said that FEAR is: False Evidence Appearing Real, we talk ourselves out of our dreams; we fulfill other people dreams by watching them and don't get paid for it. Have you ever been to a place that you haven't been before, maybe a wedding where you are seated with guests you don't know, a new job, church, or school? How did you feel? Are you in a place now that you haven't been before? What is that place?

<u>Problem in the Text:</u> : God did not come to seek the good but that which was lost; did not come to condemn the world but through Him the world may be saved; a man had to lose his life. "Greater love has no one than to lay down his life for a friend." (John 15:13)

<u>Solution to the Text:</u> Christ is love; 1 John 4:7-8 says: "Beloved let us love one another for love is of God. He who loveth not, knows not God for God is love."

<u>Solution to the World:</u> You can't be around people who are not trying to go where you are going. In this season, you must be around people who will

help you and push you into your destiny. Affirm your-self in God's Word. Turn negativity into positivity. As a man thinketh so is he. Perfect love cast out fear I John 4:18

Words to Chew On: There are people who watch things happen, people who wonder what happened, and people who make things happen. Those people who make things happen, recognize that the assign-ment on their life is not all about them, but about those who will come after them; they are willing to pass through "unchartered waters" a place they've never been before. (Greater is He who lives in me than He who lives in the world) At the opening of my business, I had four students (but prepared and set up as though it was forty students), I heard, "This is only the beginning of what is to come. Don't despise small beginnings." The steps of a good man are ordered by God. Commit your plans to the Lord and they will succeed. Turn fear into faith.

Prayer: Holy Spirit by your power move fear from me. I bind up the spirit of fear and lose the spirit of courage. Thank you that greater are you in me than he that is in the world. Amen.

Day 27

HYPOCRISY

Song: "Holy Spirit Rain Down"-Alvin Slaughter

Scripture Reference: Acts 5:1-11

But a man named Ananias, with his wife Sapphira, sold a piece of property, 2 and with his wife's knowledge he kept back for himself some of the proceeds and brought only a part of it and laid it at the apostles' feet. 3 But Peter said, "Ananias, why has Satan filled your heart to lie to the Holy Spirit and to keep back for yourself part of the proceeds of the land? 4 While it remained unsold, did it not remain your own? And after it was sold, was it not at your disposal? Why is it that you have contrived this deed in your heart? You have not lied to man but to God." 5 When Ananias heard these words, he fell down and breathed his last. And great fear came upon all who heard of it. 6 The young men rose and wrapped him up and carried him out and buried him.

7 After an interval of about three hours his wife came in, not knowing what had happened. 8 And Peter said to her, "Tell me whether you[a] sold the land for so much." And she said, "Yes, for so much." 9 But Peter said to her, "How is it that you have agreed together to test the Spirit of the Lord? Behold, the feet of those who have buried your husband are at the door, and they will carry you out." 10 Immediately she fell down at his feet and breathed her last. When the young men came in they found her dead, and they carried her out and buried her beside her husband. 11 And great fear came upon the whole church and upon all who heard of these things.

Problem in the World: It's very possible to read the Word of God and not understand it, and also possible to read the Word and not do as it says. Many Christians are busy putting their feet on someone's neck and busy trying to take the speck from someone else's eye and not remove plank from their own. Matthew 7:1-5 Everything works for you, but no one else can do what you do even though you know the Word.

Problem in the Text: Ananias and Sapphire were husband and wife. They were bringing goods to the Apostles. Ananias half sold his property and gave half to the apostles by laying it at their feet. He tried to appear spiritual before the apostles and the church.

so the Lord killed him instantly. God wanted to show that he has to be reverenced. Later the wife comes, three hours later, to the apostles. Peter asked her point blank if she and her husband sold the property for a particular amount and she said yes. Without hesitation and not knowing that her husband had died also, she lied. Ananias and Sapphira tried to appear more spiritual than they were; concerned about looking good to the apostles and the church and not concerned about what God thinks.

<u>Solution to the Text</u> The death angel came for the husband first, and then the wife.

<u>Solution to the World-</u> "Not everyone who says to me, 'Lord, Lord,' will enter the kingdom of heaven, but the one who does the will of my Father who is in heaven. 22 On that day many will say to me, 'Lord, Lord, did we not prophesy in your name, and cast out demons in your name, and do many mighty works in your name?' 23 And then will I declare to them, 'I never knew you; depart from me, you workers of lawlessness.' We try to make it look like we have it all together.

<u>Words to Chew</u>: Stop playing the religious game! I encourage to really get to know Christ. and let His power rain down and take those ways from us.

<u>Prayer:</u> Father, thank you that you know my rising and my sitting my going and my coming out. Before a thought is off my lips you already know what I am thinking. Forgive me for trying to fool man. I know I can't fool you because you see all and know all. Let the rain of your presence fall on me. Give me a complete and sincere change.

Day 28

HOLINESS

<u>Song:</u> "We Are Standing On Holy Ground" Bill and Gloria Gaither

<u>Scripture Reference:</u> Exodus 19:10-15; Galatians 5:19-21

10 ...the Lord said to Moses, "Go to the people and consecrate them today and tomorrow, and let them wash their garments 11 and be ready for the third day. For on the third day the Lord will come down on Mount Sinai in the sight of all the people. 12 And you shall set limits for the people all around, saying, 'Take care not to go up into the mountain or touch the edge of it. Whoever touches the mountain shall be put to death. 13 No hand shall touch him, but he shall be stoned or shot; whether beast or man, he shall not live.' When the trumpet sounds a long blast, they shall come up to the mountain." 14 So Moses went down from the mountain to the people and consecrated the people; and they washed their garments.

15 And he said to the people, "Be ready for the third day; do not go near a woman."

19 Now the works of the flesh are evident: sexual immorality, impurity, sensuality, 20 idolatry, sorcery, enmity, strife, jealousy, fits of anger, rivalries, dissensions, divisions, 21 envy, drunkenness, orgies, and things like these. I warn you, as I warned you before, that those who do such things will not inherit the kingdom of God.

<u>Problem in the World:</u> Many Christians believe it's okay to live an ungodly lifestyle: they believe that they have the right to sin habitually, particularly in the area of sexual immorality (fornication, adultery, gay/ lesbianism, rape, bestiality, incest and more). The problem is there are many unwed couples who have children together and who are living together. Sexual immorality is rarely addressed in the church but it's running rampart in the church. gambling/playing the numbers and lottery, believing in signs of the stars, drunkenness and more. Many professing Christians don't reverence the holiness God. You'd be surprised to know how many professing Christians think it's okay to wear revealing or tight fitting clothing. We justify sin as though it is right. James 4:17 says, "So whoever knows the right thing to do and fails to do it, for him it is sin." When we know to do right and we don't, that is a sin; In a conversation with a Christian,

the person admitted that they knew they were sinning and said, "I'm not ready to come out of this pit."

Problem in the Text: God delivers the Israelites from Egypt. He sets the parameters how the Israelites should come to him and how he is a holy God. He tells them how to have rightful living. He tells Moses that no one should approach Mt. Sinai because it is holy ground. They will be put to death if they do. Without holiness, no man shall see God. Moses taught the Israelites that they could not come to God in kind of way.

Solution to the Text: Christians are commanded to, "Be holy because I am holy." Leviticus 11:44 The death and resurrection of Christ allows each of us to approach Christ and take on the fruit of the Holy Spirt: righteousness, peace, and joy in the Holy Spirit.

Solution to the World: "I have been crucified with Christ," says Paul, "and I no longer live, but Christ lives in ; me" (Gal. 2:20). "seated with [God] in the heavenly realms in Christ Jesus" (Eph. 2:6). When was the last time you consecrated yourself? Do you not know that your body is the temple of the Lord: what are you allowing to enter your body, it's ear waves, and vision? What are you doing to your body?

<u>Words to Chew On:</u> II Tim 3:1-7 "This know also, that in the last days perilous times shall come. For men shall be lovers of their own selves, covetous, boasters, proud, blasphemers, disobedient to parents, unthankful, unholy, without natural affection, trucebreakers, false accusers, incontinent, fierce, despisers of those that are good, Traitors, heady, high minded, lovers of pleasure more than lovers of God; Too many Christians are guilty of having a form of godliness, but denying the power thereof: from such turn away. For this sort are they which creep into houses, and lead captive silly women laden with sins, led away with divers lusts. Ever learning, and never able to come to the knowledge of the truth. The altar of God is sacred; stop coming to God any kind of way; stop grieving the Holy Spirit. We have to be careful what we allow to enter our spirits and body because our body is the temple of the Lord.

Time out for habitual sin, time out for justifying your wrongdoing!

<u>Prayer:</u> Holy Spirit, touch me, fill me with a fresh wind of fire. Breathe on me, Oh God! Have mercy on me. Father, I recognize that I should be dead and gone right now. Thank you for not killing me in my mess. I decree and declare that I am holy because You are holy! Amen.

COUNSEL

<u>Song:</u> "Give Me a Clean Heart" Adoration N Prayze

<u>Scripture Reference:</u> I Kings 12:1-11

Rehoboam went to Shechem, for all Israel had come to Shechem to make him king. 2 And as soon as Jeroboam the son of Nebat heard of it (for he was still in Egypt, where he had fled from King Solomon), then Jeroboam returned from Egypt. 3 And they sent and called him, and Jeroboam and all the assembly of Israel came and said to Rehoboam, 4 "Your father made our yoke heavy. Now therefore lighten the hard service of your father and his heavy yoke on us, and we will serve you." 5 He said to them, "Go away for three days, then come again to me." So the people went away.

6 Then King Rehoboam took counsel with the old men, who had stood before Solomon his father while

he was yet alive, saying, "How do you advise me to answer this people?" 7 And they said to him, "If you will be a servant to this people today and serve them, and speak good words to them when you answer them, then they will be your servants forever." 8 But he abandoned the counsel that the old men gave him and took counsel with the young men who had grown up with him and stood before him. 9 And he said to them, "What do you advise that we answer this people who have said to me, 'Lighten the yoke that your father put on us'?" 10 And the young men who had grown up with him said to him, "Thus shall you speak to this people who said to you, 'Your father made our yoke heavy, but you lighten it for us,' thus shall you say to them, 'My little finger is thicker than my father's thighs. 11 And now, whereas my father laid on you a heavy yoke, I will add to your yoke. My father disciplined you with whips, but I will discipline you with scorpions.'" that he had devised from his own heart. And he instituted a feast for the people of Israel and went up to the altar to make offerings.

Problem in the World: Nowadays, people are slow to seek counsel from people who are wiser, mature, and skilled. They lean to our own understanding. We think we know better than our leaders, pastors, employers or those who experts in what they do and truly hear from God. We rebel against godly counsel which can have deadly results and can affect the lives of those around us.

Problem in the Text: As a result of Rehoboam not listening to godly counsel there were two consequences: 1) He caused his father's kingdom to be ripped from him and given to Jeroboam. 2) He caused the taskmasters to lose their lives.

Solution to the text: Had Rehoboam followed the counsel of his father's advisers, lives would not have been devastated and the people would not have turned on him.

Solution to the World: There is a way that seems right to man, but in the end it leads to death Proverbs 14:12. We have assurance that God hears us when we pray. I John 5:14 safety in the multitude of godly counsel. Take heed to the instruction.

Words to Chew On: When you have to make a life changing decision concerning any area of your life such as your business, family, or job decision, listen to advice and accept instruction, that you may gain wisdom in the future." Proverbs 19:20 So thankful that we have access to Christ who says call on me and I will answer you and show you great and mighty things that [you don't even know about] Jeremiah 33:3

<u>Prayer:</u> Father, forgive me for leaning on our own understanding and for not acknowledging you in all of our ways. Forgive me for my disobedience and those areas you told me what to do but I've leaned to my own understanding and have forsaken your instruction. I'm so sorry for being disobedient to what you have told me to do: (starting a business, starting a ministry, moving on to another job, getting away from people who can't take me to my next level..... not remaining/leaving a particular place, _____). Help me to take heed to the counsel you have given us. I give your name glory and honor in Jesus' name we pray. Amen.

Day 30

VICTORY

Song "Victory Belongs To Jesus" Todd Dulaney

Scripture Reference: Joshua 6:1-5

Now Jericho was shut up inside and outside because of the people of Israel. None went out, and none came in. 2 And the Lord said to Joshua, "See, I have given Jericho into your hand, with its king and mighty men of valor. 3 You shall march around the city, all the men of war going around the city once. Thus shall you do for six days. 4 Seven priests shall bear seven trumpets of rams' horns before the ark. On the seventh day you shall march around the city seven times, and the priests shall blow the trumpets. 5 And when they make a long blast with the ram's horn, when you hear the sound of the trumpet, then all the people shall shout with a great shout, and the wall of the city will fall.

<u>Problem in the World:</u> You've been carrying weight and wandering in the wilderness long enough. It's time for victory!

<u>Problem in the Text</u>: The Israelites wandered in the wilderness for 40 years unnecessarily; and picked up the gods of the land.

<u>Solution to the Text</u>: Therefore, since we are surrounded by so great a cloud of witnesses, let us also lay aside every weight, and sin which clings so closely, and let us run with perseverance the race laid out for us ...Hebrews 12:1

<u>Solution to the World:</u> Christ paid it all; He paid the price so we can be free.

<u>Words to Chew On:</u> Don't underestimate Gods power to give you victory in every area of your life; cut off the old life and start new; come out of bondage; the enemy is defeated.

<u>Prayer:</u> I decree and declare victory over every area of my life. Holy Spirit reign in every area of my life. Purify my thoughts, purify my mind, purify my body. Take control over me, Lord. Fill me with your Holy Spirit. I put my trust in you, I put my hope in you, I surrender all that I am and all that I'm not to you. Purge

me with hyssop. Change my heart, Oh, God! Thank you for the victory in Jesus' name. Amen.

Appendix

HOW TO OVERCOME AFFLICTIONS OF THE FLESH

1. ***Re-dedicate or Commit your life to Jesus the Christ.*** Perhaps, you have already made the decision to accept Jesus in your life, but you have strayed away from the Gospel and your relationship is not where it used to be. Perhaps, you hear the Holy Spirit drawing you to have a relationship with Him and you would like to invite Him into your heart. " Behold, I stand at the door and knock. If anyone hears my voice and opens the door, I will come in to him and eat with him, and he with me." Revelation 3:20. "Say aloud the following "Sinners Prayer." "The sinner's prayer must come from your heart and it is my hope this will help you to invite Jesus into yours. This prayer is here only as a guide. I urge you to pour out your heart to Jesus in your own words. Heavenly Father, have mercy on me, a sinner. I believe in you and that your

word is true. I believe that Jesus Christ is the Son of the living God and that he died on the cross so that I may now have forgiveness for my sins and eternal life. I know that without you in my heart my life is meaningless.

I believe in my heart that you, Lord God, raised Him from the dead. Please Jesus forgive me, for every sin I have ever committed or done in my heart, please Lord Jesus forgive me and come into my heart as my personal Lord and Savior today. I need you to be my Father and my friend.

I give you my life and ask you to take full control from this moment on; I pray this in the name of Jesus Christ." Into the Light Ministries Amen.

2. *Pray*. Ask God to reveal your area(s) of struggle. "And this is the confidence that we have toward him, that if we ask anything according to his will he hears us. And if we know that he hears us in whatever we ask, we know that we have the requests that we have asked of him." I John 5:14-15;

3. Recognize and *admit* that there is a *problem*. "If we *confess* our *sins*, he is faithful and just to forgive us our sins and to cleanse us from all unrighteousness." I John 1:9; Therefore, confess your sins to one another and pray for one another, that you may be healed. "The prayer

of a righteous person has great power as it is working." James 5:16

4. Having the Word of God in our heart and mind. (***Memorize, write, and recite scripture***) "I say then: Walk in the Spirit, and you shall not fulfill the lust of the flesh." Galatians 5:16; "You have heard that it was said, 'You shall not commit adultery.' But I say to you that everyone who looks at a woman with lustful intent has already committed adultery with her in his heart." Matthew 5:27-28;

"For the grace of God that brings salvation has appeared to all men, teaching us that, denying ungodliness and worldly lusts, we should live soberly, righteously, and godly in the present age." Titus 2:11-12; "But put on the Lord Jesus Christ, and make no provision for the flesh, to fulfill its lusts." Romans 13:14

5. ***Assurance of your salvation***. "But God, who is rich in mercy, because of His great love with which He loved us, even when we were dead in trespasses, made us alive together with Christ (by grace you have been saved)." Ephesians 2:4-5

6. ***Be filled with the spirit***. "And do not get drunk with wine, for that is debauchery, but be filled with the Spirit." Ephesians 5:18

7. Ongoing and Consistent ***Fellowship with Other Believers*** Make sure that you are in

regular fellowship with the body of Christ in a Bible believing and Bible teaching church that has the five-fold ministry. "11 And he gave the apostles, the prophets, the evangelists, the shepherds and teachers, 12 to equip the saints for the work of ministry, for building up the body of Christ, 13 until we all attain to the unity of the faith and of the knowledge of the Son of God, to mature manhood, to the measure of the stature of the fullness of Christ, 14 so that we may no longer be children, tossed to and fro by the waves and carried about by every wind of doctrine, by human cunning, by craftiness in deceitful schemes." Ephesians 4:11 "... not neglecting to meet together, as is the habit of some, but encouraging one another, and all the more as you see the Day drawing near." Hebrews 10:25

8. Seek professional therapy for yourself, your marriage, children or others if necessary! Also, seek help from deliverance ministers.

Suicide Prevention Help Line 1-800-273-8255 Available 24 hours everyday

The Crisis Text Line is another resource available 24 hours a day, 7 days a week. Text "HOME" to 741741.

WORKS CITED

Goeschel, Gary. *Christian Atheist*

Hammond, Frank and Ida. *Pigs in the Parlor: The Practical Guide to Deliverance*

Ehkerdt, John. *Deliverance and Spiritual Warfare Manual: A Comprehensive Guide to Living Free* (Charisma House, 2014)

C.S. Lewis/Charles Marshall "Integrity is what you do when no one else is watching."

The Bible. ESV Zondervan

The Drowning Man Story Truthbook

Silver, Nate. *Series: The Real Story of 2016-Part 10* https://fivethirtyeight.com/features/the-comey-letter-probably-cost-clinton-the-election (May 3, 2017)

Into the Light Ministries. *The Sinner's Prayer.* http://www.intothelight.org/answers/sinners-prayer.asp (1998 - 2018 Branson, MO, USA)

http://greatbiblestudy.com/bitterness.php *Root of Bitterness* (2003-2008 Robert L.)

http://www.gospelweb.net/Illustrations/TheMountainClimber.htm

CPSIA information can be obtained
at www.ICGtesting.com
Printed in the USA
BVHW07s2025151018
530260BV00001B/3/P